Praise for *Small Is Big!*

God is shifting the church from church-as-we-know-it to church-as-God-wants-it. Felicity and Tony Dale bring us a thrilling backstage account of how God is restoring divine order in his house. May the spiritual "rabbit plague" they describe here sweep through our post-man-made church world and invite all of us to join the King, Jesus, as he builds his church.

WOLFGANG SIMSON
Author of Houses That Change the World *and* The Starfish Manifesto

I have read many books on the house church movement, but this one was the most helpful of all! Tony and Felicity Dale have been involved in the house church movement, both in England and in the United States, for many years and bring a wealth of information and practical help in every aspect of house church ministry. *Small Is Big!* will be the first book I will be recommending to those who are led to get involved in simple church.

ROBERT FITTS
Author of The Church in the House: A Return to Simplicity

Tony and Felicity bring years of global leadership and experience in the simple church movement to this book. They are genuine pioneers of this movement in the West and have visionary insights to offer in this easy-to-read, practical, and big-hearted book. We are grateful for their ministry.

ALAN HIRSCH
Founding director of shapevine.com and author of The Forgotten Ways

In this new book by Tony and Felicity Dale, "rabbits" are simple churches, and those rabbits are multiplying rapidly! Here you will find quality "rabbit food" in the form of dozens of practical insights wrapped in real-life stories. Tony and Felicity Dale are wise voices speaking into this emerging movement.

JOHN WHITE
Community coach at LK10.com

Clear. Practical. Timely. The contents of this book are praiseworthy, but more importantly the book springs from the lives of a couple who are implementers rather than theoreticians, people who are Kingdom-minded and humble in heart.

CURTIS SERGEANT
Director of Global Strategies, e3 Partners Ministry

In a time that is crucial, God sent a precious gift to our nation—Tony and Felicity Dale. There are few people I respect and love as much as I do these two. It is my privilege to call them friends and coworkers. Their experience is a prophetic voice to us, and this book gives wings to that voice.

NEIL COLE
Author of Organic Church, Search & Rescue, *and* Organic Leadership

Tony and Felicity Dale ask the right question in this book: why is the church growing in Africa, Asia, and Latin America, while thousands of churches are closing and church attendance is at an all-time low in America and Europe? They ask the question and they tell us the God answer! Don't miss this book!

FLOYD MCCLUNG
International director of All Nations

Tony and Felicity Dale have found keys to restoring God's original purpose for the church. Today's church is 95 percent tradition and 5 percent truth. What if we could turn these percentages around? I encourage you to read and reap from *Small Is Big!*

SID ROTH
Host, It's Supernatural!

Tony and Felicity Dale are at the forefront of a revolution that is brewing in the body of Christ today. That revolution is marked by a growing number of Christians who are gathering outside the organized church and finding Christ in fresh ways in Christian community. This book will give readers a window into some of the exciting things that are marking this revolution. Among other things, you will discover that Jesus Christ can be profoundly known and expressed outside the typical structures of institutional Christianity in new and simpler forms of church life. Read this book and join a revolution that just might outstrip the Reformation!

FRANK VIOLA
Author of From Eternity to Here, Reimagining Church, *and* Pagan Christianity? *(coauthored with George Barna)*

SMALL
is
big

Unleashing the Big Impact
of Intentionally Small Churches

TONY & FELICITY DALE | GEORGE BARNA

BARNA
An Imprint of Tyndale House Publishers, Inc.

Visit Tyndale's exciting Web site at www.tyndale.com.

TYNDALE is a registered trademark of Tyndale House Publishers, Inc.

Barna and the Barna logo are trademarks of George Barna.

BarnaBooks is an imprint of Tyndale House Publishers, Inc.

Small Is Big!: Unleashing the Big Impact of Intentionally Small Churches

Designed by Jessie McGrath

Published in association with the literary agency of Fedd and Company Inc., 9759 Concord Pass, Brentwood, TN 37027.

The Library of Congress has catalogued the original edition as follows:

Dale, Tony.
The rabbit and the elephant : why small is the new big for today's church /
Tony and Felicity Dale.
p. cm.
Includes bibliographical references and index.
ISBN 978-1-4143-2553-8 (hc : alk. paper) 1. Church growth. 2. Small churches. I. Dale,
Felicity. II. Title.
BV652.25.D35 2009
262´.26—dc22   2009002215

ISBN 978-1-4143-3941-2 (sc)

Printed in the United States of America

17   16   15   14   13   12   11
7   6   5   4   3   2   1

To Jon, Matt, Tim, and Becky, who had no choice about coming on the journey with us.

Contents

Introduction

WE ARE IN rural India and it is hot—so hot that the sweat is dripping down our faces. The oppressive heat is compounded by the number of bodies packed into a room without air-conditioning for this conference on church planting. The women, like exotic tropical flowers in their colorful saris, brighten the otherwise drab surroundings. It has been a long day. Although we have frequently broken things up with different activities, the concrete floor gets very hard after a few hours—we, the honored Western visitors and our interpreter, are the only ones privileged to have chairs. It's time for some light relief.

"Imagine you take two elephants . . ."

The audience perks up. They sense a story is coming.

"For our purposes, they are a male and a female."

Small titter.

"And you put them in that room behind us" (pointing to a tiny kitchen off the main room).

More laughter. They know you couldn't possibly fit one elephant into that room, let alone two!

"You give them plenty to eat and drink and you shut the door on them. Three years later, you come back and open the door. What comes out?"

A number of people call something out. We look to our interpreter for help.

"They say that three elephants come out. Mom, Dad, and a baby."

"That's good. In three years, Mom and Dad elephant have had one baby! Now, instead of two elephants, let's pretend you put two rabbits in the room."

They start to chuckle. Already they can anticipate what is coming.

"At the end of three years, when you open the door, you had better run for your life, because millions of rabbits will explode out of that door."

The room erupts in laughter!

But they have also caught the point. Something that is large and complex is hard to reproduce. Something that is small and simple multiplies easily. Elephants take a long time to reach maturity and have a long gestation period. It takes time to reproduce a single elephant. Rabbits, on the other hand, are extremely fertile all the time. They reach maturity in four to six months, and their gestation period is a mere thirty days. Hence the expression "breed like rabbits."

We learned this story from others,[1] but it doesn't matter where in the world we go—from primitive rural India to the sophisticated cities of the West—people relate to the analogy and instinctively apply it to church planting.

God always intended for His church to multiply. Although multiplication starts slowly, it is infinitely more effective than addition in the long term. Churches that are intentionally small (simple churches, organic churches, house churches) can reproduce easily and with virtually no cost. They have the potential for rapid multiplication because anyone can gather a few people together in a living room or coffee shop. And they are very easy to duplicate. Not only that, but they also penetrate sectors of society that will never enter a church building. That's why small is big!

Jesus is building His church. Across the nations, the proliferation of intentionally small churches is having a major impact. Let's follow Jesus into the harvest, make disciples, and see multiplying families of His people transform our world.

1

IN THE BEGINNING

CHARLES DICKENS BEGINS his novel *A Tale of Two Cities* with the haunting phrase "It was the best of times, it was the worst of times. . . ." For us, these words had become an overwhelming reality.

We arrived in the United States in 1987 with high hopes and great expectations. We had come from the concrete jungles of London's East End to the wide-open spaces of Texas. We had left behind a cold, rainy, windblown island for the balmy temperatures and sun-filled days of the Texas hill country. We loved the food, enjoyed the people, liked the city. Our four kids reveled in the unrestricted access to the outdoors and a swimming pool to share with their new friends. It was indeed the best of times.

It was also the worst of times. God had abandoned us—at

least that's what it felt like. He had led us to move to Texas, but as soon as we arrived at the airport, it seemed like He deserted us and took the next plane back to England, leaving us to fend for ourselves!

How could we have come to this?

We had met at the prestigious "Royal and Ancient Hospital of Saint Bartholomew" (Barts Hospital, founded in 1123). It was love at first sight over the histology microscope. That's not quite true, but because there were so few Christians in the school (just 4 of us out of 150 students in our class), we were constantly thrown together, and a deep friendship developed. We soon sensed God leading us to get married.

By this time, England was already post-Christian, so all of the believers in the medical school and hospital—everyone from nurses and medical students to physical therapists and janitors and even a few of the qualified doctors—formed a close-knit community. Because we all spent so much of our time together—studying and working at the hospital—we gradually came to the realization that we were functioning more as a church within the hospital than we did as members of the traditional churches we each attended on Sunday. So we decided to take the unlikely step of actually calling ourselves a church. This was a highly controversial move at the time. Everyone expected church to be run by professionals. However, it did give us the dubious satisfaction of a certain notoriety, as we were thrown out of the organization that united student Christian groups across the nation and preached against from some of the best-known pulpits in London!

And God began moving. Our times together were often glorious examples of how the Holy Spirit can move in a group of people who are looking for Him to lead. Soon, students started coming from all over the country to see what was happening, and they used the spiritual fire they experienced to ignite similar moves back in their own colleges and universities. As a result, more people became Christians and many were filled with the Holy Spirit.

After we received our medical degrees, our medical school church sent us out, along with a wonderful nurse, to start a new church in the East End of London. We were joined by a great couple that we had met when we moved there. At that time, London's East End was not the gentrified place it is now. It was a very socially deprived area with devastating problems everywhere we looked. But Jesus seemed to shine even more brightly in the darkness.

In his practice, Tony often heard harrowing stories that really had no medical answer, and when he did, he would simply say to the patient, "You know, I'm not sure that medicine can help you with this situation, but have you ever thought of praying about it?" The patient would typically respond, "Oh, doctor, I pray, but I feel like my prayers just hit the ceiling!" This was Tony's opportunity to share the Good News! Hundreds of his patients became believers, and many miracles occurred right there in the office as he prayed for their healing or deliverance. As the church there grew, Tony was able to refer new believers to a home group that met right on their street—or at least very close to where they lived.

Please don't think that we were anything special. What we were seeing was not unusual. In fact, these kinds of stories were happening all over the country. Set against the backdrop of the charismatic movement, England was an exciting place to be a Christian during the 1970s. Churches were spontaneously starting in people's homes, giving rise to what was referred to as the "house church movement." Thousands of these churches sprang up, giving every little town and village in the country a dynamic expression of the body of Christ.

Those were exhilarating times. Some days we literally ran to the building we were meeting in because we couldn't wait to come into the Lord's presence. Occasionally the presence of God was so real that we would all find ourselves facedown on the floor, lost in adoration of Him. We wouldn't dare go into a meeting with unconfessed sin because we knew that the Holy Spirit would most likely expose it publicly.

Across the nation, streams of these house churches were forming. They had their own apostolic leadership (early attempts to model Ephesians 4 leadership teams), and sometimes thousands of believers came together for glorious weeks when we lived in tents and experienced amazing times of worship, teaching, and fellowship.

Like most of the house churches across the United Kingdom, our ambition was to grow as large as possible. The concept of the megachurch was just beginning to gain acceptance, and we assumed that a big church was the indication of God's approval. Our little group grew rapidly, eventually becoming one of the largest shows in that part of the city. Like most of the other house churches, we had long since outgrown a home. But as we grew bigger, subtle changes occurred. Gradually the sense of Jesus' presence dimmed. In reality, the majority of nonconventional churches had become little more than souped-up versions of all the other churches around.

In the spring of 1987, we were on a plane returning from California, where we had been ministering. One of us turned to the other: "Has God said anything to you while we have been away?" As we compared notes, we discovered that He had told both of us individually that we were to leave England and move to the United States. He subsequently made it plain that our destination was to be Texas.

Six months later, the day after the first hurricane to hit England in five hundred years and the day before Black Monday when the stock market crashed, we, our four kids, and twelve of the largest boxes the airline would allow arrived in Texas. We didn't know a single person. We felt like Abraham, who obeyed a call to move not knowing where he was going.

For the first few years we lived in America, we tried to fit into good local churches. We failed abysmally—mostly due to our lack of understanding of American church culture.

Finances became a problem. We had naively assumed that we were supposed to be working for the same ministry Tony had been involved with in London: a ministry to doctors and people in the medical and allied professions. That, too, failed spectacularly. And nobody wanted to employ two unlicensed physicians.

But the most devastating thing was that God stopped speaking to us. He didn't give us any indication of why. We spent time repenting and seeking His face, but the heavens were silent. It just appeared as though He wasn't there any longer. God had abandoned us.

This went on for nine very long, very dark years.

During those years we had lengthy conversations in which we mulled over what we had seen in England. We eventually came to the conclusion that, although we hadn't realized it at the time, we had probably lived through a period of revival. We spent hours discussing the nature of church. Was there something about church as we were seeing it in the United States—or even what the house church movement in England had become—that somehow militated against the free flow of the Holy Spirit? Why had we experienced such a powerful move of God in the early years, and why had it stopped? Could the sense of God's moving in power have had anything to do with the fact that the churches were small—small enough to have deep fellowship?

As we tried to answer these questions, we asked our British church-leader friends what they might do differently if they could do it all over again. One of them answered with disarming honesty, "I would just get together with a few friends over a drink at the pub to talk about Jesus and what He is doing." Then he added wistfully, "But I can't do that; I have too many church responsibilities."

We also reflected on the nature of revival. Why did some revivals—like the Welsh Revival—appear to end so quickly, while others—like Methodism under John Wesley—seemed to last for many years? What about the growth of the church in China, arguably the largest move of God the world has ever seen? Could it be that when new wine is put into new wineskins, the revivals carry on for decades?

As we thought about this and studied the Scriptures, our theology of church began to change. We realized that we needed to view the New Testament through the lens of a small group setting in order for it to make sense. How can you bear one another's burdens (Galatians 6:2) or teach and admonish one another (Colossians 3:16) in a congregation of five hundred when you may not even know the person sitting next to you?

What does it really mean to love one another and prefer one another in love (Romans 12:10)?

Rather than someplace to go on Sunday mornings, church in the New Testament was a vibrant community of Jesus followers, a 24-7 Kingdom lifestyle. Church was simple, taking place over meals and based on relationships. The people considered themselves to be "all members of one body" (Ephesians 4:25, NIV). They were family.

We wondered how this relational way of life pulsating with the presence of the Holy Spirit could have been reduced to the spectator sport it is in most churches today. In some congregations, people barely know each other's names, let alone what is really going on in each other's lives. What needed to change for us to recapture the vital community those early believers shared?

We studied Acts 2 and saw that in the very first days of the church, all the believers met together and shared everything they had. They worshiped together at the Temple each day, met in homes for the Lord's Supper, and shared their meals with great joy and generosity—all the while praising God and enjoying the goodwill of those around them.

But following the martyrdom of Stephen, persecution forced these new believers to scatter, which further spread the gospel. After this, apart from one reference to Paul teaching in the school of Tyrannus, every mention of church is in reference to a group of people meeting in their homes. As we looked into church history, we found that this pattern continued for just under three hundred years until around AD 321, when the emperor Constantine made Christianity the official religion of the Roman Empire.

We discovered that the Greek word used in the New

Testament for "church" is *ekklesia*. It was not a religious word—in fact, it is the word used to describe a rioting mob or a civic assembly, as in Acts 19. Although the word literally means "those who are called out or called forth," the best New Testament scholars agree that it also means a gathering or meeting of people. As Frank Viola describes in *From Eternity to Here,*

> *The word meant a* local *community of people who assemble together regularly. The word was used for the Greek assembly whereby those in the community were "called forth" from their homes to meet (assemble) in the town forum to make decisions for their city. Consequently, the word also carries the flavor of every-member participation in decision-making. . . . It's a* community *of people who* gather *together and who possess a shared life in Christ. As such, the* ekklesia *is visible, touchable, locatable, and tangible. You can visit it. You can observe it. And you can live in it.*[1]

In contrast to His emphasis on the Kingdom, Jesus only spoke of church on two occasions that are recorded in the Gospels. The first is in Matthew 16 after Peter's great declaration of faith, "You are the Christ, the Son of the living God." Jesus' response is this: "You are Peter, and on this rock [this revelation] I will build My church, and the gates of Hades shall not prevail against it" (Matthew 16:16-18).

Then in Matthew 18, Jesus discusses how to handle sin in the life of a believer, and He says if the person who is sinning will not listen when you go to him with a witness, you are to take it to the church. He continues,

*Whatever you forbid on earth will be forbidden in heaven,
and whatever you permit on earth will be permitted
in heaven. . . . If two of you agree down here on earth
concerning anything you ask, my Father in heaven will
do it for you. For where two or three gather together as my
followers, I am there among them.*
—MATTHEW 18:18-20, NLT

Could this last sentence be the simplest definition of church? Does it matter whether we meet in a house or office building or the local Starbucks or even in a church building? As long as two or three are gathered, don't they form the basic building block of church?

A national survey conducted by The Barna Group at the close of 2007 revealed that most Americans are surprisingly open-minded about what a church really is. When asked to determine whether each of several activities represented "a complete and biblically valid way for someone to experience and express their faith in God," substantial majorities of the public accepted some of those options as legitimate forms of church. Those included engaging in faith activities at home, with one's family (89 percent embraced that as biblically valid and complete); participating in a house church or simple church (75 percent); attending a special ministry event, such as a concert or community service activity (68 percent); and participating in a ministry that meets at a place of employment (54 percent). Indeed, tens of millions of Americans are comfortable with the idea that you can participate in God's church without having to attend a worship service in a building constructed for religious activities.[2]

When disciples come together, Jesus is in their midst, but

this is not the same as Jesus living within the individual believer. There is another dynamic at work when we are in the company of others—Jesus says that He is present among us.

The New Testament writers used the word *ekklesia* to refer to God's people coming together in His presence in various ways. The first describes a church that meets in someone's house (Romans 16:5; Colossians 4:15). The second refers to a church in a specific city, like the church in Jerusalem (Acts 15:4) or the church in Corinth (1 Corinthians 1:2). Finally, the word is used to describe what has become known as the "church universal," all believers everywhere throughout the ages (Ephesians 1:22-23).

As we thought about how we use the word *church* today, we realized that the meaning has changed. Most commonly, the term is used to describe a building or congregation, such as First Baptist Church or New Life Fellowship. But these are not biblical uses of the word. In fact, when the word is used to describe a denomination like the Methodist Church or the Catholic Church, one could argue that this is actually anti-biblical, since it has the effect of dividing the body of Christ (1 Corinthians 1:12-13).

Small, multiplying groups of believers are known as house churches, simple churches, organic churches, or missional communities. The terms are used interchangeably, but all refer to simple, vibrant communities of believers who are meeting in homes, offices, campuses, or wherever God is leading them. For the sake of discussion in this book, we'll primarily use the "simple church" label.

All of this study was changing our theology of church. But now we were faced with an even bigger question: What were we going to do about it?

2

GOD BREAKS THROUGH

FINALLY, IN THE SPRING OF 1996, after nine years in God's wilderness training school, we had come to the end of our rope. We delivered God an ultimatum—this is not a course of action we recommend, but by this stage we were desperate. "Lord, if You haven't changed things by Christmas of this year, we are going back to England, whether we hear from You or not!" At least there we could earn a reasonable living.

Things soon began to change. God began speaking to us again. And the first thing He said was, "You will be part of a move of My Spirit a second time." We desperately wanted to believe this. Could God be about to visit His people? Would we experience His presence and power again?

For years, we had been crying out to God, asking that He

would give us a business idea that might provide a reasonable income. A few months after our ultimatum, He answered that prayer in a most unusual way. Tony required surgery following a basketball injury, and was so shocked by the medical bills we received that he decided to look into the whole foundation of medical pricing. Almost overnight, we had a workable concept on our hands and started the Karis Group,[1] the business that now supports us. It has since grown to the place where we are able to travel and be involved in whatever Kingdom ventures we sense the Lord wants for us.

Earlier, while trying to make ends meet, we had been involved in a marketing company where we had become acquainted with large numbers of not-yet-believers. We invited some of the leaders to our home for pizza and a discussion on business principles.

"We'll base our discussions on a book written by the wisest man who ever lived," we told them.

So about a dozen of us gathered once a week for pizza followed by a discussion on the book of Proverbs. Our times together were interactive and free flowing. No one taught; there were no right or wrong answers. We just discussed the Scriptures together. Our times were always very lively, with much laughter and good-natured banter. There was even one outstanding evening when two of the guys who had come out of the drug culture quite solemnly discussed the idea that perhaps some of their drug deals had gone bad because they weren't following the principles in Proverbs!

Over the course of the next year, each member of the group surrendered his or her life to a God who loved them unconditionally and accepted them as they were.

At that time, we were still involved in a traditional church that met about half an hour's drive from our home. However, when that church moved to a location that was twenty minutes even farther away, we went to the senior pastor and asked him what he recommended. He proposed that we start a church.

We had always somewhat resisted that idea, but he used an argument that fully persuaded us.

"Statistics show that the best means of evangelism within an American context is starting a church," he said.[2]

At that stage, two of our kids were still at home, and we knew we needed to do something for them. We decided to start what we called a "breakfast Bible club." We suggested that our kids invite all their friends from our neighborhood for breakfast and some spiritual activities. We chose a Sunday morning to do this because we figured that the Christian kids would be in church, and we wanted to reach the non-Christians. We prepared a huge breakfast—bacon and pancakes and breakfast tacos—and the kids started coming. They came for the breakfast but they stayed for the Bible-based interactive activities. They, too, started to give their lives to Jesus. As the kids' lives changed, a few of their families wanted to know why, and they asked if they could join in too.

When we finally combined the two groups in our modest-sized home—the businesspeople and the breakfast Bible club—we had over fifty people overflowing from our living room into the kitchen and hallway and up the stairs. It was magnificent chaos!

What were we going to do? The obvious option was to rent a building and start a traditional form of church. But we had had nine years on the backside of the desert to consider church, and our perceptions of what church was all about had changed. We were also hearing stories from places like China where God was evidently moving in awe-inspiring power by multiplying small churches that met predominantly in homes.

As we pondered the matter, we considered a number of reasons that seemed to indicate that we, too, should multiply small churches rather than seeking to get larger.

1. Jesus ministered in homes, and much of the Gospel narrative takes place in homes. Jesus ate in people's homes, healed in people's homes, and taught in people's homes (Matthew 8:14-15; 9:10, 23-25, 28).

2. New Testament Christians primarily met in small group or home settings. When the apostles went to a town, they often preached in the synagogue. But it usually did not take long before they were thrown out and forced to move on to more intimate home gatherings (Acts 18:4-7). And the New Testament includes numerous references to the church in someone's home (Romans 16:5).

3. It is difficult to obey the commands of the New Testament in groups that are too large. For a very instructive study, look up the more than fifty "one anothers" of the New Testament. It would be difficult to edify one another (Romans 14:9), serve one another (Galatians 5:13), and confess our sin to one another (James 5:16) in a large group context. Spiritual transformation is more often the result of close-knit relationships.

4. Jesus entrusted His church to ordinary, untrained men (Acts 4:13). Those with no formal religious training can easily start a church in a home.

5. Most aspects of ministry are better in a small setting. For example, 1 Corinthians 14:26 says that when we come together each person should be able to bring a contribution, whether it be a song or a teaching. This would be much easier to accomplish in a small group than in a large congregation.

6. Simple churches multiply more quickly. We want to see rapid growth of the church, but building programs and pastoral training can be very time consuming. Simple churches can multiply with negligible cost and at a very rapid rate. We saw this demonstrated in countries such as India, where, even in this very poor nation, hundreds of thousands of churches have been started over the last decade.

7. Simple churches allow all the members of Jesus' body to be fully functioning (Romans 12). This occurs best within the intimacy of a smaller setting where people are not intimidated into silence by the size of the gathering.

We were aware that churches that embody these values could meet in all sorts of places—hospitals, retirement centers, factories, outdoors. (This is part of the reason we now prefer to use the term simple or organic rather than house church.) We also realized that meeting in a home would not automatically prevent us from being at least as traditional as the church that meets in the building with the spire.

But it was apparent to us that God is clearly working to restore the body of Christ in this generation in a different way. Even though His hand of blessing can be seen in many traditional churches, the Holy Spirit seems to be nudging people everywhere toward something smaller and more organic.

So we decided to embark on an adventure of discovery with God. We were going to multiply small churches.

At this point, we made the first of many mistakes that we have made along our simple-church journey. (We can illustrate the many ways how not to do church from the mistakes we have made!) We split the church in two. For more than a year, people complained that they felt like they had been through a divorce. Now we understand that a better way to have handled this situation would have been to birth a daughter church around a newcomer.

But in spite of our mistakes, we slowly began to add churches to what we now saw as a "network." Our personal preference was to work with groups of not-yet-believers, although other Christians did join us. We became aware of others around the nation thinking in similar ways.

We also had the opportunity to travel and experience firsthand what have now become known as "church planting movements"—rapidly multiplying churches with the ability to transform a nation. The first place we visited was Mozambique. Tony had gone to school with Rolland Baker, who with his wife, Heidi, was now ministering to the poorest of the poor in that nation. Following the news of devastating floods, Tony flew over to see what he could do to help. The United Nations flew his team by helicopter to wherever a group of people had gathered on higher ground, and along with giving medical care and providing food, the team also preached the gospel. A simple presentation often resulted in the whole community finding Christ. A few months later, we returned there as a family and found that the work was accelerating. This has continued, and now Iris Ministries helps to care for more than ten thousand churches, there and in other nations, led by pastors they have trained.

We also witnessed another church planting movement in India. God seemed to be doing something even more amazing there. In 1992, Victor Choudhrie, a renowned cancer surgeon and dean of a reputed medical school, heard God's call to leave medicine and plant churches. With no theological background and no church planting experience, Victor was forced to study the only textbook he knew on the subject: the Bible—specifically the Gospels and the book of Acts. Now, a decade later, as a result of Victor and his wife Bindu's obedience, more than ten thousand churches have been started, reaching one hundred thousand people.

In 2009, Victor decided he wanted to give the Lord a "birthday present" of one hundred thousand baptisms on the Day of Pentecost (the birthday of the church). When the final numbers came in, they totaled more than two hundred fifty thousand baptisms on one day. And there are many others like Victor Choudhrie across India. This is apostolic work, the ascended Christ building His church.

On our first trip to India we met Wolfgang Simson. Wolfgang is an anointed and outspoken German church-growth specialist who has made a study of simple churches around the world. His book *Houses That Change the World* (rereleased in 2010 as *The House Church Book*) has arguably been the most influential piece of modern writing on this subject.

We invited Wolfgang to visit us in Texas and sent out a few e-mails letting friends know he would be speaking in our home. It wasn't long before we began to suspect that a few more people would be turning up than we had anticipated. We borrowed chairs from everyone we knew and arranged for caterers. Fortunately by this time we had moved into a larger home to accommodate our expanding business. It has an extensive open-plan area, which is just as well because more than 160 people turned up. (The one thing we had not thought through was the septic system—but that is another story!)

Wolfgang inspired and challenged people with his stories of what God was doing with simple churches around the world and his exposition of the Scriptures as the basis of what we were experiencing. But perhaps as important as what he said were the relationships created that day. Rather than any kind of organization, these relationships, along with others that have been forged since, form the foundation of much that is going on in the simple church movement in this country.

In the fall of 2000, Jim Mellon and David Underwood, both leaders of other simple church networks in central Texas, approached us. "We've had this idea for a magazine about what God is doing with these new churches," they said. "Would you like to join us?"

We thought it was a great idea! We had already seen the way in which God often uses magazines during moves of His Holy Spirit.[3] And so *House2House* was born. Initially a printed magazine, it is now primarily a Web site. It has been a huge and humbling privilege to work with House2House and share the stories of people from all over the country and the world.

We realized that we had been given the opportunity to

witness a move of God unfolding in front of our eyes. We knew that we were watching history in the making.

And speaking of history, there is much that we can learn from previous moves of God.

3

A HISTORY LESSON

Picture the scene. The year is 1536. Near Brussels, Belgium, in a town called Vilvoorde, stands a fortified castle. It is a cold October dawn. A large crowd has gathered outside the castle walls; a heretic is to be executed.

The gates of the castle open, and a small procession crosses the bridge under which the river Senne sleepily flows. The frail prisoner, his complexion pale from eighteen months spent in jail, stumbles between two burly soldiers. They come to a halt before the crowd. The charges against the condemned man are read: "You have been found guilty of infringing the imperial decree that forbids anyone to teach that faith alone justifies."

The executioner binds the prisoner to the stake, a hempen noose around his neck; brushwood is piled high around him.

The prisoner does not struggle, but he suddenly cries out with a loud voice, "Lord, open the King of England's eyes!" Immediately the executioner snaps tight the noose that takes the prisoner's life from him, then lights the fire that consumes his body.

William Tyndale, the father of the English Reformation and the apostle of England, has died for preaching salvation by faith alone.[1]

The crowd is quiet. They have just witnessed the triumph of a martyr.

Before his death, William Tyndale (c.1494–1536), a scholar, linguist, and priest, had one life-consuming passion: to see the Bible translated into English so that the ordinary person could read it. In England at the time, the only Bibles available were in Latin or Greek, and therefore inaccessible to the majority of people. Tyndale vowed that his translation would use everyday English, the language of the peasants.

"If God spare my life, ere many years I will cause a boy that driveth the plow to know more of the Scriptures than the Pope." The rest of Tyndale's life was devoted to fulfilling that vow.

When his request to translate the New Testament was turned down by the church hierarchy in England, Tyndale fled to Germany. While he was there, scholars believe that he met with Martin Luther, a monk and university teacher of theology who had become convinced from his study of the Scriptures that salvation was by grace alone and could not be earned.

In Germany, Tyndale completed his translation of the New Testament from the Greek. In 1526, several thousand printed copies of the New Testament, hidden in bales of wool or packed into sacks of flour, were smuggled by boat down the Rhine and across the English Channel into England. Many of these were discovered, confiscated by church authorities, and publicly burned. Anyone found with one in his or her possession ran the risk of execution.

Why was there such opposition to the man in the street having access to a translation of the Scriptures? Those in church authority claimed that without training, people would not be able to interpret the Bible. Ordinary people were too burdened with worldly business to understand Scripture correctly and therefore could not be trusted with it. Because it was in Latin, only the clergy could read it and explain it to the people. The Bible was viewed as the property of the church, a book to be read only at public services and explained solely by the priests.

Following the printing of the New Testament, the English church authorities condemned Tyndale as a heretic and demanded his arrest. His next few years were spent living in poverty on the run—but working now on the Old Testament as well. Finally, in 1535, someone posing as a friend betrayed Tyndale, and he was captured and imprisoned. He was charged with heresy, and his priesthood was publicly stripped away. Even so, the quality of his life was such that his jailer and other members of the jailer's household were converted.

William Tyndale's final prayer was answered. In August 1537, less than a year after Tyndale's death, King Henry VIII gave his permission for what had become known as the Matthew's Bible to be published. It did not have William Tyndale's name in it (to keep from embarrassing the government), but approximately 90 percent of the work in this version was his. Most of it lives on even today in the 1611 King James Authorized Version.

The invention of the printing press enabled the English

version of the Bible to spread widely and quickly. England had been waiting for this, and it was like floodgates opening.

It was a wonderful thing to see. Whoever possessed the means bought the book and read it or had it read to him by others. Aged persons learnt their letters in order to study the Holy Scriptures of God. In many places there were meetings for reading; poor people dubbed their savings together and purchased a Bible, and then in some remote corner of the church, they modestly formed a circle, and read the Holy Book between them. A crowd of men, women, and young folks, disgusted with the barren pomp of the altars, and with the worship of dumb images, would gather round them to taste the precious promises of the Gospel. God himself spoke under the arched roofs of those old chapels or time-worn cathedrals, where for generations nothing had been heard but masses and litanies. The people wished, instead of the noisy chants of the priests, to hear the voice of Jesus Christ, of Paul and of John, of Peter and of James. The Christianity of the Apostles reappeared in the Church.[2]

Obviously there is more to the history of the Reformation than the somewhat simplistic idea of biblical truths being made available to the person in the pew. The historical Reformation of the sixteenth century was the result of a number of factors acting synergistically to produce a seismic shift in the religious landscape of Europe. It was in part a reaction to the corruption in the Catholic Church of that time and in part the product of political aspirations.

However, no matter what the ignoble motives of some of the key players may have been, at its root, the Reformation was initiated by an emerging spiritual awareness of the truth that salvation comes from faith alone—that it cannot be purchased with money given to the church or earned by good works.

The invention of the printing press helped spread these ideas across the nations. As Clay Shirky says in his book on the social and economic effects of the Internet, *Here Comes Everybody: The Power of Organizing without Organizations*:

> *Two things are true about the remaking of the European intellectual landscape during the Protestant Reformation; first, it was not caused by the invention of movable type, and second, it was only possible after the invention of movable type, which aided the rapid dissemination of Martin Luther's complaints about the Catholic Church . . . and the spread of Bibles printed in local languages. . . . Because social effects lag behind technological ones by decades, real revolutions don't involve an orderly transition from point A to point B. Rather, they go from A through a long period of chaos and only then reach B. In that chaotic period, the old systems get broken long before new ones become stable.[3]*

Fast-forward a few centuries. How is this history lesson relevant to us, nearly five hundred years later? Simply this: the Reformation was the result of a grassroots change in theology produced by ordinary people having access to the Scriptures in their own language through the new technology of the day—the printing press.

At various times in history, seismic changes have occurred. These changes have not been gradual or planned. Instead, they represent the convergence of ideas and technology in such a way that a dramatic shift of opinion, a genuinely new way of looking at things, emerges. What most people just see as sociological change is actually the God of history advancing His Kingdom.

A shift with the potential impact of the Reformation is happening in the Western church today. And this time it is occurring as the church—instead of the Bible—is being put back into the hands of ordinary people.

The objections are similar as well: how can untrained and unqualified people run churches? That should be reserved for the professional clergy. People who have jobs don't have the time to prepare a sermon, let alone get trained in hermeneutics. How are they going to prevent heresy? On what basis do they claim the authority to act as the church? Are they accountable to any higher church authorities? Can ordinary people administer the sacraments?

Just as the Bible in the heart language of the people empowered the ordinary believer in Tyndale's day, simple church today allows ordinary men and women to "be the church" rather than "go to church."

These disruptive changes—significant jumps in technology and understanding converging over a short period of time— represent societal change that in times past may have taken decades to occur, but now can happen extremely rapidly. The Internet, social networking sites,[4] and the emergence of simple church concepts worldwide could only grow at this rate at such a time as this.

Ideas can be profoundly powerful. And ideas as they relate to

God's truth have the potential to move far beyond the confines of the church. As in the book of Acts—or in the Reformation— God's people have the power to actually transform society (Acts 17:6).

A reformation—a tsunami as big as that of the Reformation of Tyndale's day—is occurring.[5]

4

HISTORY BROUGHT
UP-TO-DATE

THIS RE-FORMATION OF church and society is not new. In one sense, it is as old as the early church of New Testament times.

For the first two or three centuries after Pentecost, the church met mainly in homes, and laypeople were responsible for those meetings. The believers shared meals, prayed for one another, and simply lived life together. However, by the end of the first century, an elite leadership was beginning to emerge. A massive shift occurred when the emperor Constantine made Christianity the official religion of the Roman Empire in AD 321. Overnight it seemed, Christians changed from being a persecuted minority to a favored majority. Over the next few decades, church buildings were erected, a privileged clergy status was formed, and the church service became the center of Christian culture.

And for the past seventeen centuries, church has been an event to attend. Most Christians go to a special place at a special time to watch special people perform. Once or twice a week, they sing a few songs, listen to a monologue, put money in the offering plate, and go home.

But throughout history, people have also chosen to meet outside the four walls of the traditional church.[1] And many moves of God have started primarily in homes. A more recent example of this would be the Jesus Movement of the late 1960s and 1970s. This was mostly made up of new converts who were saved and then met outside of the institution in homes or intentional communities. Although this particular movement died out, many of the movements that started in homes eventually became the denominations of our day; they did not have a theology of multiplying small gatherings. They had not realized the megapower of the microchurch.

One of the most notable of these moves in modern history is the house church movement in China.

During the late 1940s, when Mao Tse-tung came into power in China, the Communist government determined to purge the nation of the religion he believed was used to promote Western imperialism. Missionaries were driven out, and many Christians were killed or imprisoned. But rather than wiping out Christianity completely, Mao's efforts simply drove the church underground. Despite the very real threat of persecution, imprisonment, torture, and even execution, ordinary believers—primarily women and teenagers—left their homes to lay down their lives and preach the gospel. Small gatherings of believers meeting in secret multiplied rapidly.

Today the church in China is exploding, though not through

large buildings and powerful preachers. It is estimated to have grown from one million believers in the middle of the last century to more than one hundred million today.[2]

Currently, the simple church movement is developing rapidly in countries all around the world. And the West is not being left out. We are no longer just sitting on the sidelines wistfully watching God work in the rest of the world.

In the 1970s, a handful of Christians in the United States began deliberately meeting in their homes, mostly in reaction to the problems they saw in the traditional church. A decade or so later, another wave of home churches started. These early pioneers were convinced that this was the scriptural way to meet. Both groups were dismissed as irrelevant by the religious world. But no one could have guessed what transformation would occur within the Western church in subsequent years.

In the mid- to late-1990s, a third wave of simple churches began, and this group of people had a far more pragmatic outlook: "God is doing something remarkable across the world," they said. "Could it be that He wants to do something similar here as well? Let's follow the Holy Spirit's leading and see what happens." As it turned out, God was doing something here, too.

Wolfgang Simson became convinced of this as he analyzed the findings of his research. His studies suggested that the fastest growth in the church was not occurring where churches were getting ever larger and more prosperous. Instead, the most rapid growth seemed to be occurring in small churches led by ordinary believers. In 1998, Simson posted 15 Theses for the Reformation of the Church, the principles behind this extraordinary growth, on the Internet—a technology similar in its potential to change the world today to the printing press in its day.[3]

Since it began, this current wave of church growth has gathered momentum until now the idea of simple church is generally accepted by much of the religious establishment as a viable way of "doing church." Some denominations have started a simple church track, mainstream publishers are accepting books about the movement, and secular organizations are recognizing it as a true social phenomenon. Publications such as the *Los Angeles Times* and *Time* have even produced articles exploring the trend.[4]

The scale on which this is occurring would have been inconceivable just a few years ago. Studies in 2008 and 2010 by The Barna Group estimate that about six million adults attend some form of simple church each week. Somewhere between ten and fifteen million adults are estimated to visit a house church each month.[5] Only God could have engineered such a massive hunger in the hearts of His people, so that a traditionally conservative group like Christians would experiment on so large a scale with these newer forms of church life. Because of the incredible numbers of people involved, we have chosen to refer to this occurrence as a movement.

The traditional resistance to these microchurches has dissolved rapidly in recent years. A national survey among the senior pastors of conventional Protestant churches—the "competition," if you will, for organic forms of faith—showed that there is widespread acceptance of such forms of ministry. In that survey two-thirds of the traditional pastors (65 percent) said they felt that house churches "are legitimate Christian churches." In addition, three-quarters of them (77 percent) said they believed that when people in house churches convened, they "genuinely worship God." In fact, two-thirds of these pastors went so far as to admit that "a house church might be a better spiritual fit for some people than a conventional local church would be." While pastors of conventional churches expressed reservations about the levels of spiritual accountability of organic church participants, there is certainly a refreshing openness on their part to the possibility that God can work in any setting where people's desires and intentions are appropriate.[6]

LEAVING THE LEGACY

People are leaving traditional churches—or "legacy churches" as our friend Kent Smith likes to call them in reference to the values they have imparted to us—in vast numbers. Thousands of Western churches are closing their doors every year,[7] never to reopen. Many pastors are leaving full-time ministry each month.[8]

At first glance this may appear to be a tragedy, and indeed, for many who make their living in ministry, it is a time of great stress and hardship. But is it possible that something more significant is going on? Could the Holy Spirit be behind this shift? Could God be on the move? Could this profound dissatisfaction with the status quo actually be a Holy Spirit–inspired recognition that the Christian walk is more than a monotonous duty? Could it be that we are actually on an epic journey, a glorious adventure with a God who will not be confined to our predictable boxes?[9]

Could God be moving us outside the walls of our church buildings (and our homes) to where the pain and needs—and people—are so that we can be channels of Jesus' love to a world that is hurting and in desperate need?

Those who are leaving the church are not necessarily immature in their faith. Many, in fact, have had a long-standing walk with the Lord and have even been in church leadership.[10]

Although some people leave and do nothing, many are seeking to serve the Lord or work in the Kingdom in ways they found impossible within the four walls of the building.

In his book *The Present Future*, Southern Baptist leader Reggie McNeal outlines the problem when he states, "A growing number of people are leaving the institutional church for a new reason. They are not leaving because they have lost faith. They are leaving the church to preserve their faith."[11]

Is it any wonder that many of those who are leaving traditional structures find themselves gazing longingly at the simplicity of New Testament home churches and asking, "Can I do that?" For many, the answer is proving to be a resounding yes! And the result is "church outside the box," a small gathering of friends loving Jesus together and reaching out to the community around them.

House2House[12] speaks to this new movement. On a daily basis, House2House receives phone calls and e-mails from people all over the country. The most common comment goes something like this: "God led us to start a meeting in our home (or office or the local coffee shop). We thought we were the only ones with this crazy idea until we came across your Web site. Now we realize we are not alone!" Everywhere we go, we meet people to whom God has whispered the same idea.

The phenomenon that is occurring in front of our eyes is a *re*birthing of the church—God is taking an event-based institution and re-forming it so that it is becoming life- and relationship-based. It's interesting that He is not merely transforming the old—patching the old wineskin—but He's birthing something with a new heart and a different DNA than we have seen in our lifetimes.

No longer tied to special buildings, simple church is

spilling over into homes, businesses, college campuses, and coffee shops—anywhere life occurs. It is being led by an army of ordinary men and women who are daring to believe in a God who unconditionally loves them and delights to partner with them in His Kingdom.[13] The focus is no longer on professionals and programs, but rather on enabling every-member ministry. Instead of precious resources being used internally to maintain staff and buildings, they are now being used to fund missions and mercy ministries to a world looking for a relevant church.

Perhaps one of the most notable features of this re-formation is the understanding that ordinary people can be trusted to listen to God and respond to His leading. We are no longer dependent on someone with special training or abilities to hear from God on behalf of the people. We all hear and obey God, and we understand that the Lord Himself will build His church and grow His Kingdom. The Holy Spirit is the Spirit of truth, and He will guide us into all truth (John 16:13).

Please do not think this is a criticism of individual legacy churches. We personally owe a lot to the legacy churches of our formative years, and we are thrilled that one of our four adult children is still seeking God with his whole heart at a wonderful legacy church. We believe that God continues and will continue to use legacy churches in remarkable ways.

But it does appear that God is also doing something new. There is no location, no city or town to which one can travel to find the center of this movement. There is no superstar whose conferences we can attend. But all across the nation, the Holy Spirit is speaking to His people. And everyone seems to be hearing the same thing: church as we know it has changed. Many believe this current move of God will prove similar in scope and impact to the Reformation of the sixteenth century.

Today, God seems to be saying that we can be "church" in all manner of different and unusual ways. Many people are starting churches in their homes or places of work. Others are reaching out specifically to those who have never been a part of a legacy church—making disciples and bringing them together in vibrant communities where they can express their newfound faith in Jesus.

We've found great liberty in following the principles of simple church—freedom from church politics, from a need to "perform," and from we-have-always-done-it-this-way tradition. In simple church, we no longer struggle to please people but are now free to march to the Holy Spirit's drumbeat. Liberated from endless meetings, we have time to get involved in our communities and to reach out to a world that so desperately needs the Lord.

Many who object to the idea of simple church are using some of the same kinds of arguments used by those who opposed William Tyndale's translation of the Bible into the common language of the people. But God is overturning these preconceived ideas, and the monopoly of the professional clergy is being broken as the Holy Spirit is putting the church back into the hands of His (ordinary) people.

To put it simply, simple churches allow ordinary men and women today to "be the church." This is not a political revolution but a shift in spiritual understanding with the power to transform society.

5

BEYOND REFORMATION

SOME GOOD FRIENDS of ours have been involved in a network of simple churches since the early 1990s. For some years, several of the men in the group have been meeting regularly every Monday night for prayer. They used to meet in one of their homes, but a few months ago, they sensed that the Lord wanted them to move the meeting so they could actually pray "in the harvest." They chose the local Starbucks as their new venue. Almost immediately things started to happen as other customers noticed what they were doing. Within two weeks, one of the regular customers at that Starbucks became a Christian through their gathering! Every time the group met, the men had the opportunity to get to know someone new. Today, there are around twenty-five new believers because the men's prayer group moved to Starbucks, and two groups meet there weekly. Sometimes onlookers will ask for prayer, and the men never hesitate to get up to lay hands on people and minister in the gifts of the Spirit.

Ray, one of the original members of the prayer group, leads a ministry that supplies food to all the organizations helping the poor in town. When the Starbucks manager found out about this, he invited Ray to take their leftovers every night to distribute to the poor. All of this is occurring because the prayer meeting moved out of a home and into the harvest.

Simply changing the structure or location of the church, however revolutionary it might seem, is not an end in itself. God is after far more than this. He wants a body of people that is dependent on Him and that will follow wherever the Holy Spirit leads. He wants us to go beyond re-formation of the church to transformation of society. If the deck of cards has merely been shuffled—if people are leaving traditional structures simply to meet more informally in homes—it will do little to advance the Kingdom of God.

But what if God is using this simple church movement to prepare an army of ordinary people who will invade their world with the Good News of the Kingdom and thereby become radically effective in their communities?

THE GOSPEL OF THE KINGDOM

Jesus was very focused on His Father's Kingdom, speaking about it more than any other subject. The Gospels include more than a hundred references to the word *Kingdom*. Jesus preached about it (Luke 4:43) and told people to seek it above all else (Matthew 6:33). He told parables about it (Matthew 13; 25) and said that the Kingdom was near to people who were healed (Luke 10:9).

Jesus spent the forty days between His resurrection and His ascension discussing the Kingdom with His disciples (Acts 1:3). For a subject so central to Jesus' thinking, it is amazing we pay so little attention to it!

Perhaps the best definition of God's Kingdom comes from the Lord's Prayer:

Your Kingdom come, Your will be done on earth as it is in heaven.

At its simplest, the Kingdom is anywhere the will of God is being done. It is the realm of the rule and reign of a loving God. Although Jesus revealed the Kingdom by healing the sick and releasing captives (Luke 4:18-19), the Kingdom is primarily spiritual rather than physical (John 18:36). Entrance to the Kingdom is free, yet it costs everything. The principles governing this Kingdom are described in the Sermon on the Mount and are best summed up in the great commandment to love the Lord your God with all your heart, soul, and mind and to love your neighbor as yourself (Matthew 22:37-39).

This Kingdom of God is an upside-down kingdom. It takes the world's values and exposes them for what they are: hollow and superficial. And then it sets its own standards: up is down, death leads to life, law is transformed by grace, the poor are rich, leaders serve, and the humble are exalted.

The Kingdom expands when the Good News is preached to those who are currently in the kingdom of darkness. As people respond to the gift of God's love by surrendering their lives to the King, they gain access to the Kingdom. Being born again of the Spirit conveys more than just citizenship in a kingdom, however. It also includes sonship in a royal family (John 1:12).

The disciples experienced the Kingdom of God during the three years they spent with Jesus. They watched Him demonstrate its principles and listened to Him teach about it. After Pentecost they naturally lived out what they had seen and heard. They ate in one another's homes, took care of people's needs, fellowshipped together, prayed for each other, and remembered Jesus' teachings (Acts 2:42-47). They referred to this lifestyle as church: a local and visible expression of the Kingdom on earth. And like yeast in dough, it spreads through society.

LIQUID CHURCH

Until recently, the church has played a central role in Western society. Recent writings refer to the traditional church as "solid" church because it is like a block of ice: a solid structure within a community that meets in a physical location at a specific time each week.[1]

Church leaders seek to attract people to the events going on in the church building itself, relying on the fact that being part of a local congregation is already central in their society's value system. But people no longer believe that it is necessary to go to church in order to be socially acceptable.

In his book *The Forgotten Ways*, Alan Hirsch writes:

> *In Australia we have the somewhat farcical situation of 95 percent of evangelical churches tussling with each other to reach 12 percent of the population. And this becomes a significant missional problem because it raises the question,*

"What about the vast majority of the population (in Australia's case, 85 percent; in the United States, about 65 percent) that report an alienation from precisely that form of church?" How do they access the gospel if they reject this form of church? Because it is clear from the research in Australia . . . the 85 percent ranged from being blasé ("good for them, not for me") to total repulsion ("I would never go there").[2]

Intensifying the problem we face in our new missional context, the long-term research conducted by The Barna Group predicts that by 2025 the local church will lose roughly half of its current "market share," and alternative forms of faith experience and expression will pick up the slack. With these statistics in mind we understand why, in America, traditional church structures are only likely to appeal to 35 percent of the overall population.

But what happens when the block of ice that is traditional church melts? The water is no longer contained in a solid form, and it begins to flow freely. A number of writers are now identifying a very different type of church that, like water, is seeping into every crack and crevice of our culture. Liquid church[3] happens when we stop inviting others to come to church and instead we go out into every sphere of society as the Lord leads. We reach out to our neighbors or our coworkers, and instead of asking them to come to church, we get together with those people right where they live or work. In this way, segments of society that might never have experienced church life are affected by the Kingdom of God.

A great example of this comes from some friends in Georgia.

David Havice, the senior pastor of a traditional church, was led by the Lord to transition his church into a network of simple churches. Two years into the process, he had a network of five or six churches but found himself without much to do—he no longer had a job description! With a desire to reach out at a personal level, he pondered what other community he could connect with. He had always loved motorcycles, so he bought himself an old Harley-Davidson and started hanging out with a group of bikers who congregated at a local café. There is now an organic church, formed from the harvest of that group and meeting at that café. The owner of the café helps to lead the new church. The bikers responded to a fellow biker in a way they might never have responded to a minister.

When people become believers within the traditional model of church, they usually join that congregation and are soon involved in everything that is going on. After a short time, they are no longer friends with anyone who isn't a Christian. After someone has been a Christian for a year or two in this kind of a context, the chances of that person leading another person to Christ are slim.

A person who has just given his life to Jesus is excited about his faith and wants to share his experience with everyone he knows. If we remove him from his friends, we have lost a great opportunity to reach out into a new circle of people. (Obviously there may be rare times when it is better for a person to stay away from old friends—such as if the new believer is an alcoholic whose friends hang out in bars. But even so, God might want the new believer to try to reach out to his friends first, trusting the Holy Spirit to protect him, while he deliberately trusts God to give them the chance to also experience the transformative nature of the Gospel. In Mark 5:18-20, Jesus sent the Gerasene demoniac straight back to his friends and family, and the man told all the people in the city what Jesus had done for him.)

Jesus described the Kingdom as yeast in a lump of dough (Matthew 13:33). The yeast spreads virally until all of the dough is changed. In the same way, this movement from a traditional, attractional model of church life to a simple, liquid model is a vital part of the transformation that is currently occurring. And it has the same potential to permeate our society.

6

A RADICAL (CHURCH) LIFE

A FEW YEARS AGO, the Lord gave a vision to Michael, a good friend of ours. In it, Michael saw crowds of people waiting in line to see what appeared to be a glass case in a museum exhibit. The display consisted of an exquisite lidded container, superbly crafted and yet simple and elegant. Everyone was marveling at its delicate workmanship, captivated by its beauty.

There was just one problem. The people were in awe of the container. They had missed the fact that the container held a priceless jewel of surpassing worth.

The same danger exists for us today. This is a book primarily about the container. But simple church is just that—a container. The priceless jewel is Jesus Himself. He is our pearl of greatest price, the focus of our existence, the One we love and adore. Our chief end is to worship Him. Our aim is to be His body: "Jesus with skin on." We want Jesus' love to spill out of the container and onto everyone around us, especially those in the gutters of life who are crying out for help. Simple church is merely a container that helps us to see Jesus more clearly and enables us to reach out to those who need Him most.

Jesus is far more interested in our hearts than He is in our pursuit of correct doctrine or the right church structure. All who know Jesus as Lord are the body of Christ, no matter which spiritual family they may belong to (1 Corinthians 12:12-13). Jesus and His family—no matter where and how we choose to worship—are far more important than the ability to justify an ecclesiological position.

THE VALUES THAT DEFINE US

In these days, God is moving in many different situations. In some places that focus on the healing power of God, extraordinary miracles are occurring.[1] Other movements are concentrating on praise and worship.[2] Still others have produced 24-7 prayer initiatives.[3] Any of us who think that we have all the answers or that we are "where things are really happening" are merely deluding ourselves. A synergy occurs when we lay aside our differences and work together across the body of Christ.

However, it does seem that the Holy Spirit is currently bringing an increasing focus onto the values that define us as a body of His people. And since the structure of church is determined by its values, there is an apparent emphasis on that, too. If we think that "big is beautiful" when it comes to church, then we will tend to have a more corporate structure, as opposed to small groups that operate like family.

According to the Old Testament, the children of Israel committed spiritual adultery by giving allegiance to the gods of all the nations around them (Jeremiah 3:8-9). "We would never be that foolish," modern-day Christians assume. But we of the church era have done no better. Christians in the West have followed the gods of the American dream, of materialism, of popularity, of numbers. We have become performance driven rather than love motivated. We give Jesus the title of "Lord," or "Head of the Church," but in reality, we devise our own plans and then ask Him to bless them. We build buildings and create programs, following the advice of church-growth statisticians, and then we expect the Holy Spirit to come in power. And when, in His great mercy, He delights to bless us through some of these things, we presume that we have built His dream church. How can we have fooled ourselves so badly?

In other parts of the world people may literally be laying down their lives because of their trust in Jesus. In some states in India an automatic three-year prison sentence is the punishment for people who are caught baptizing or being baptized. If someone becomes a Christian in many Indian villages, he or she may not be allowed to use the communal well and may have to purchase rice from a neighboring village. On one visit to India, we met five girls, teenagers ages fifteen to nineteen, who spent their weekends traveling miles on foot from village to village, telling anyone who would listen about the Kingdom of God and the power of Jesus to transform lives. We wonder what it will take for us to share a similar passion. As we experience more of God's love, a delight to communicate it with others comes naturally.

In another nation we visited, new believers may literally be martyred because of their faith. They will certainly be ostracized by society, get thrown out of their homes, have difficulty getting jobs, and may be imprisoned. When people have to pay a high price for their faith, they have a far deeper commitment to Christ.

Becoming a Christian costs us very little here in the West—and our Christianity is often correspondingly shallow. Obviously we do not wish for persecution, but maybe we could ask God for more passion. Where is the church that Jesus died for? Where is the spotless bride for whom He laid down His life? Our response to His love is our reckless obedience.

NON-RELIGIOUS CHRISTIANITY

One of the concepts that was very important to us during the move of the Spirit in the United Kingdom is what became known as "non-religious Christianity."[4] This kind of spiritual life cannot be put into a box or placed on an agenda. It cannot be programmed or reduced to a curriculum. As Wolfgang Simson likes to say, "Programs are what the church resorts to when the Holy Spirit leaves."

It has been a guiding principle for us that anything we help to start, whether it be a church or a ministry like House2House, should never have enough structure that it can survive without the active input of the Holy Spirit. Consider this example: The first church we ever helped start was the group that met in London while we were in medical school. Some years after we had been sent out from that church to start another church in a very poor section of London, we were contacted by the leaders of the original church. "We are not sure what has changed," they told us, "but we feel as if the presence of the Lord is not really in the gatherings anymore. What should we do?" As we asked them what they thought their next step should be, they told us, "Well, you always taught us that there should never be enough structure that the church can survive without the presence of God. Maybe we just need to let it go." And to their credit, that is exactly what they did. As a result, members scattered to many other churches across London and became blessings in many new places, rather than propping up something that God wanted to fall into the ground and die (John 12:24).

All too often, we cheapen Christianity to the point that it becomes a religion of rules in which dos and don'ts (particularly the don'ts) govern our lives. In an effort to please God by being separate and not loving the world (2 Corinthians 6:17; 1 John 2:15), we often live by a rule book rather than trusting that God has indeed transformed us from the inside out. When our spiritual walk is based on obligation and duty ("This is what a good Christian should do"), it eventually leads to a dull, lifeless religion, or even more devastatingly, drives people away from the Lord altogether. Most people in the West were brought up in shame-based families and/or churches. "People are going to hell. Therefore you should preach the gospel." This reasoning is guilt based. Although it sounds spiritual, it implies "Christ died for you and you are doing so little for Him? You are guilty! You ought to try harder." It attempts to shame us into doing more.

There is no question that the gospel should be preached. But what motivates us to do it? The grace and love of Jesus operating inside us causes us to want to do what legalism or shame-based religion says we ought to do. When we become alive in Christ, He transforms us from the inside out. We find ourselves motivated by His life within. He gives us new desires. What was drudgery under the old system becomes life under the new. Paul could say, "The love of Christ compels us" (2 Corinthians 5:14). Jesus said, "My yoke is easy and My burden is light" (Matthew 11:30).

This is not to say that we always "feel" like doing what is right. Love is not a feeling; it's an act of the will. The Bible is clear that we are to live by the life of the Spirit within (Galatians 5:25). To live according to the Spirit will result in living according to the Scriptures.

If we are genuinely new creations (2 Corinthians 5:17), we can live in the freedom of following the Spirit within us. When we were born again, God gave us new hearts with His laws written on them, not a set of commands to live by (Hebrews 8:10). For the Christian who is seeking to follow God, doing right comes naturally! Christianity is a way to live from the Source within, rather than dutifully conforming to a set of outward patterns of behavior acceptable to the establishment.

When our faith becomes legalistic, it only confirms the world's view that God is carrying a big stick and waiting to catch the unwary in some unsuspected sin. One church building near our house often displays a "verse of the week" on a large sign out front. Most of the time, these verses are harsh and condemning. Whenever we drive past, we wonder who would be interested in that kind of a God, especially if He only speaks in King James English. Jesus reserved His harshest criticisms for the legalists of His day. As Paul wrote, "the letter kills, but the Spirit gives life" (2 Corinthians 3:6).

The gospel is Good News! God loves us unconditionally—so much that He entered human history to bring us back into relationship with the three-in-one Godhead. The carpenter from Galilee has always been immensely attractive and winsome to the seeker of truth. May our lives, too, be attractive and winsome to others because we genuinely love them. May the Lord deliver us from being modern-day Pharisees!

God wants His church back. Enough of man-made programs and plans; simple church is all about Jesus! He is the Head and we, the church, are His body (Ephesians 4:15-16). As His body, we (both simple and legacy church) need to repent of following our own plans and ideas rather than His vision for His people. Not a casual, shallow, "God, I'm sorry for what others have done," but a profound identification with His body and a pleading that He will have mercy on us and visit us again with His grace and power. Our quest is for a 24-7 experience of the presence of God, rather than an expectation that we somehow fulfill our religious obligations by turning up to certain meetings. As we fall in love with Jesus all over again, we naturally seek God's will for us as individuals and for our churches and give Him sovereign authority over His body.

As we go to battle against the principalities and powers, we will see captives set free in the name of Jesus. How is it that for most Christians, spiritual warfare is little more than a concept, rather than a reality? We once heard someone put it this way: "If you have never met the devil face-to-face, maybe it's because you're going in the same direction!"

When Jesus gives us gifts of knowledge and healing we will see the supernatural happening, as the Word becomes flesh and dwells among us (John 1:14). As we yield the direction and control in our meetings to the Holy Spirit, we will watch in awe as He orchestrates everything according to His divine plan for us.

Simple church is built on these principles of non-religious

Christianity. We are no longer interested in conforming to the status quo. Rather than simply toeing the religious party line, we long to follow the inner promptings of the Holy Spirit both individually and corporately. Just imagine a people with their hearts on fire and a church that consistently seeks God's face, learns His will, and then obeys it. God could transform the nations with such a people.

7

THE MASTER'S VOICE

IF SIMPLE CHURCH is all about following Jesus, then one of our foundational skills has to be an ability to hear from God. Jesus said that He only did what He saw the Father do and only spoke what He learned from the Father (John 5:19-20; 8:28). Although we, too, want to hear and follow the Father, many times we do not know how to hear God. This may be because we have always relied on others—a pastor, conference speaker, or writer—to listen to God for us.

There is really only one way to learn to hear His voice, and that comes through intimacy with Him. John 17:3 states, "And this is eternal life, that they may know You, the only true God, and Jesus Christ whom You have sent." As we become utterly sold out to Jesus—knowing Him, spending time with Him, losing ourselves in His presence, and basking in His love—we can learn to recognize the whisperings of the Holy Spirit in our hearts as He speaks to us.

If you've been married for any length of time, you could probably be in a room with a hundred people all talking at once and still recognize your spouse's voice. This is because you've spent much time together, enjoying each other's company, sometimes even to the point of thinking the same thoughts simultaneously or finishing each other's sentences. Jesus wants to have a relationship with every one of His children that is even more intimate than that between a husband and wife. He does this through His Holy Spirit.

Although Jesus was fully God when He walked on this earth, He chose to lay down His deity (Philippians 2:6-7). John the Baptist told the assembled crowd that the Holy Spirit would characterize the ministry of Jesus (Mark 1:8), and he was correct. In fact, Jesus did not even begin His public ministry until He had been empowered by the Holy Spirit (Luke 4:14), and after that, everything He did was in the power of the Holy Spirit (Acts 10:38).

In the same way, Jesus told His disciples that it was better for them that He go away because then the Holy Spirit would dwell within them and lead them (John 16:7, 13-15). The same Holy Spirit who empowered and led Jesus wants to lead us. He is the Paraclete—literally "one who is called alongside." He brings glory to Jesus by revealing the things of God (John 16:14-15). As we cultivate our relationship with the Holy Spirit, we find ourselves pleasing God and knowing His will (Romans 8:8-9, 14).

As we joyfully surrender to the Lord, we will surely pick up His heart and passion for the lost (John 3:16-17; 2 Peter 3:9).

God is intensely missional, and as we spend time in His presence asking to see life from His perspective, He will break our hearts with the plight of those who do not know Him. He then gives us authority over the works of the devil so that we see signs and wonders done in His name (Mark 16:17-18; 1 John 3:8). The purpose of these is that people put their faith in the saving power of Christ. Abiding in Christ results in great fruitfulness, for without Him we can do nothing (John 15).

Reformation occurs when the whole body, individually and corporately, learns to know God in a deep and impacting way, recognizing His voice when He speaks to us.

> *The sheep hear his voice; and he calls his own sheep by name and leads them out. And when he brings out his own sheep, he goes before them; and the sheep follow him, for they know his voice.*
>
> —JOHN 10:3-4

RECOGNIZING GOD'S VOICE

Our God is a communicator.[1] John 1:1 states that in the beginning was the Word, and the Word was God. Communication is part of His very nature. He is constantly speaking to His people; He has not hit the mute button!

Felicity used to do a lot of counseling. In order to reduce the time spent in counseling, she would pray prior to each session and then write down the thoughts that came into her mind about that person's situation. Thoughts often seemed to come from left field, but she wrote them down anyway.

About 85 to 90 percent of the time, when Felicity went back and reviewed her notes, the things that she had written down—the things that she thought the Lord had shown her—were accurate. On one occasion, a girl with depression came for counseling, and the Lord had already told Felicity that the girl's father had abused her. So it took only two questions to find the root of her depression: "How was your relationship with your father?" and "Did he abuse you in any way?" (Notice she didn't immediately ask if the father had abused her. The girl needed a way out if she didn't want to talk about it. Besides, Felicity might have been wrong!) That exercise taught Felicity to trust the Lord to speak to her through that "thought out of nowhere" as she prayed. She was learning to recognize His voice.

Perhaps the most common way God speaks is through our thoughts. In our experience it is very rare to actually hear God speak audibly. As we cultivate an attitude of listening, we learn to distinguish His voice from the jumble of our own thoughts.

As we look at the Bible, we find that God speaks in a number of other ways to His people.

God's Word

Psalm 119:105 says, "Your word is a lamp to my feet and a light to my path." Down through the ages, the saints of God have been guided by His written Word.

Shortly after Tony was baptized with the Holy Spirit,[2] he attended a meeting where the Lord was powerfully healing people. Some with obvious back problems were free from pain; people with arthritis were finding their joints immediately loosened following prayer. The person leading the meeting joked, "If there are any doctors here, they'll be looking for a new job." Tony was in medical school at the time, and this shook him to the core—he had never asked the Lord if being a doctor was what God wanted for his life. In turmoil, he went back to his room and he sensed the Holy Spirit asking him, "Are you ready to follow Me even if it means leaving medical school?" The next morning, when Tony opened the Word for his regular Scripture reading, he found the Lord challenging him from the words recorded in Micah 2:10 (NASB): "Arise and go, for this is no place of rest." The written Word was confirming the word already spoken into his heart. Experiences like this have helped to convince us that the Bible is our final plumb line against which any other word from God is measured.

Tony did leave medical school for two years, until God clearly told him to return. This may be one of the only times that Tony believes he literally heard the Lord's voice. He was working within a hospital pharmacy at the time, just cleaning some of the bottles used for intravenous infusions, when out of the blue he heard the Holy Spirit say he was to go back to medical school. Immediately he doubted that this was really the Lord's voice. So he asked the Lord to confirm this in ways that Tony couldn't influence. God answered his prayers that the medical school would let him return without having to repeat any of the courses he had already completed, and that the government would give him back his original grant money, both of which are unheard of in the United Kingdom.

The peace of God

Colossians 3:15 speaks of the peace of God ruling in our hearts. The word *rule* here literally means to "act as umpire." A deep, internal peace is often a way God reveals His will. For example, a few years ago our business took a serious downturn when our primary client suddenly decided to terminate our services. After the initial panic, an amazing peace took over. Although it took almost a year to find a replacement customer, God's peace assured us He was in control and all would be well.

Dreams and visions

In both the Old and New Testaments, God frequently spoke to people through dreams and visions. Peter, quoting the prophet Joel, said that dreams and visions, along with prophecy, would now characterize the people of God.

> *And it shall come to pass in the last days, says God, that I will pour out of My Spirit on all flesh; your sons and your daughters shall prophesy, your young men shall see visions, your old men shall dream dreams. And on My menservants and on My maidservants I will pour out My Spirit in those days; and they shall prophesy.*
> —ACTS 2:17-18

Jesus' earthly father, Joseph, was guided by a dream to leave Bethlehem and go to Egypt in order to save Jesus' life (Matthew 2:13-14). A vision gave Peter permission to go to the home of Cornelius, a Gentile, and led to the revelation that God was extending salvation to the Gentiles as well as the Jews (Acts 10). A vision also guided Paul to Macedonia to preach the gospel (Acts 16:9).

We have seen this at work in our own lives too. One night, Felicity dreamed that a course we were offering in our home was available online. Over the next few months, we did the necessary work to make it available on DVD and CD; it has since blessed many more people than we could have possibly reached in our own home.

A leader of one of the local home churches had a dream about one of her neighbors who was not a believer. When she saw that woman the next day, she was able to share the dream with her. This opened up a dialogue between the two of them, and the neighbor soon became part of that church.

Prophecy

Prayer is us speaking to God, and prophecy is God speaking to us—through someone else. Prophecy usually serves to confirm something that God is doing or saying. In 1 Corinthians 14, we are told to pursue love and to earnestly seek the spiritual gifts, especially that we may prophesy. We're also given guidelines for using prophecy safely—for edification, encouragement, and comfort (verse 3). These are safe boundaries for the exercise of this gift. Prophecy in this context is not for predicting the future or convicting someone of sin. It is simply for sharing the impressions we have from the Lord. It is also safer if we do not try to interpret the prophecy that the Lord gives us for someone else—we should let the Holy Spirit do that.

Godly counselors

Finally, according to Proverbs 15:22, the Lord often uses the words of godly counselors to speak to us. Many times we have benefited from the wisdom of others. When first considering how we should go about having our books published, it was through the wisdom given to us by our own local simple church that we initially went the self-publish route.

SEEING GOD AT WORK

In the Gospels, we read that Jesus not only spoke what He heard the Father saying, He also only did what He saw the Father doing. How do we see what God is doing? Just as hearing God's voice involves recognizing when He is speaking through our thoughts, seeing Him involves realizing that He may speak through the pictures of our imagination. But it is more than that.

Let's say that one of your coworkers mentions a problem he is having at home. You offer to pray for him, and God answers your prayer. This is God at work too! When we introduce God into a situation through prayer in Jesus' name, He will answer in ways that bring the Father glory.

In one rapidly expanding church planting movement overseas, more than 80 percent of the new churches have been started as a specific result of answered prayer. Church planters pray for the needs of a local family and God answers. The story about what has happened spreads far and wide. Those who are interested then gather to hear the gospel. Some believe and a church is started in that home and that village.

As individuals and as churches, we can learn to recognize what the Father is doing and saying. In the current simple church movement, this is happening more and more.

A good friend of ours, John White, gathered a group of people with the express purpose of learning to hear God's voice. When the group (church) gathered, its members would share what they were hearing from God and how they planned to obey. Over the course of a year, five people in the group heard the Lord tell them to start new churches. In a recent e-mail,

John described two of the churches formed from that original church:

> *One of the members of the original group is the head wrestling coach at a Lutheran high school. He heard the Lord tell him to see his wrestling team as a church. Each day, as he listened to the Lord, he received instructions as to how to do this. And each day as the team met for practice, the coach would share what he was hearing from God. He began to teach the wrestlers how to hear from God for themselves and about the nature of church. (They joked that this was a church that really believed in the "laying on of hands"!) After the season was over, a coach from another sport remarked, "Your team is the only team in the school that is really a family. How did you do it?"*
>
> *Another member of the original group is an ex–police officer who lives in a rural area outside the city. One day a stray dog showed up in his yard and stayed around for several days. The owner of the dog turned out to be a registered sex offender who had become a follower of Jesus but was treated as a social outcast by the community. The ex-cop heard the Lord say to him, "Invite this man and his wife for dinner." Out of this meal together grew a church with four couples. This home church has become the only place where this former sex offender and his wife have normal relationships with other people. Recently, the ex-cop was in tears as he told of how transparent and life-changing this group has been for every couple involved.[3]*

Ordinary people are hearing God's voice, going out into the marketplace, and seeing God work in unusual ways. As they bring what they hear from Him to the group of people they meet with, the body is built up. And as the church waits on the Lord and discovers the mind of Christ (1 Corinthians 2:16), Jesus is building His church.

8

DRENCHED IN PRAYER

THE TEMPERATURE WAS several degrees below freezing; our sparsely furnished hotel room was unheated. We decided to leave early for the weekly all-night prayer meeting in the hopes of getting warm. Arriving at least an hour before the meeting was scheduled to begin, we found the building (which seated about ten thousand people) packed out—women with babies on their backs, children sleeping on the floor, old people, young people— and everyone worshiping. We didn't understand a word of what was going on, but when the meeting started, everyone began to pray loudly as the Lord led them, crying and shouting out to God. They stood, hands raised, some with fists clenched, tears running down their cheeks. It was profoundly moving. Forty minutes later, someone rang a bell and the praying stopped. Then another topic was announced, and off they went again.

It continued like this all night. We felt humbled, as though we were only in kindergarten as far as prayer was concerned.

Over the next few days, we met several people who had fasted for forty days, and many who had seen amazing miracles in response to prayer. By the end of our time at the Full Gospel Central Church in Seoul, Korea (at that time, the largest church in the world),[1] it was clear that we were watching a mighty and deep movement of the Holy Spirit in response to the fervent prayers of His saints.

Before our visit there in 1983, we had naively assumed that a church of that size (around 350,000 at that time) had to be superficial—a mile wide and an inch deep. How could a church grow that quickly unless there was some kind of superstar or fantastic "show" to which people were responding in droves? We were wrong! God works wherever His people seek Him with all their hearts.

We went to their "prayer and fasting mountain." Hundreds of people, wrapped in sleeping bags because of the cold, had come here to pray and fast as they waited on God. Some were sick and were praying for healing; some had business problems; some were praying for friends or relatives; others were praying for God to transform the nation.

Our conclusion? This was a place where God was profoundly moving. Thousands were finding Christ, and it was all related to prayer.[2]

Any ongoing move of God is totally dependent on prayer and intercession. The simple church movement has been birthed in prayer by the many people in both simple and legacy churches across the nation who have been asking God to take back His church. But if this movement is not nurtured on our knees, it could rapidly go off course or simply fizzle into nothing. We cannot expect a move of God to come cheaply; we must be a people who are willing to pray the price.

Today's move of God will flourish as intercessors storm heaven and do battle on their knees against the very real spiritual forces arrayed in opposition to us. It needs people who will cry out to God, asking Him to do something of such incredible magnitude that only He can get the glory. Any movement thrives as those gifted by God wait on Him hour after hour, day after day until He comes in power. Although it may sound spiritually glamorous, fasting and intercession is actually a hard, hidden work. Frequently it seems as though the heavens are as brass and our prayers don't get any higher than the ceiling. The fruit of these times, however, is more than we have even dared to imagine in terms of answered prayer and seeing God move in power.

Some years ago we were asked an interesting question. If we were given a choice between a powerful movement of God that was filled with signs and wonders and resulted in thousands of Christians being touched by the Holy Spirit and a slower, steadier evangelistic or missional work that brought thousands of not-yet-Christians into the Kingdom and transformed a society, which would we prefer? Our answer had to be the latter, just as we had seen on our visit to South Korea.

Saddleback Church pastor Rick Warren once interviewed Dr. David (Paul) Yonggi Cho (leader of the Korean church we just described) about church planting. Cho said that when he first began his church, he had to pray for four to five hours each day in order to conduct spiritual warfare and maintain fellowship with the Holy Spirit. Now he has been able to cut it down to three hours![3]

In another interview by Brother Denny Kenaston of *The Heartbeat of the Remnant* magazine, Chinese church leaders reported that most of their leaders pray for two to three hours a day, although some spend their whole day in prayer. Many nights, they said, the whole church fasts and prays together, and sometimes by morning, the floor is slippery because of the tears that have been shed.[4]

David Watson was involved for fourteen years in North India with a church planting movement that saw over forty thousand churches started. For the past four years David has been involved in training church planters in Africa who have started more than five thousand churches. He writes:

> In a recent meeting of the top one hundred church planters in our ministry, we looked for common elements among these high producing leaders. Each of these church planters, along with the teams they led, started more than twenty churches per year. One group started more than five hundred churches in the previous year. The only common element we found in all these church planters was their commitment to prayer. There were other common elements, but the only element that was present in every team was a high commitment to prayer.
>
> These leaders spent an average of three hours per day in personal prayer. They then spent another three hours in prayer with their teams every day. These leaders were not all full-time religious leaders. In fact, most of them had regular jobs. They started their days at 4:00 a.m., and by 10:00 a.m. were at work.
>
> These top performers also spent one day per week in

fasting and prayer. The whole team spent one weekend per month in fasting and prayer.[5]

One of the most powerful prayer times we have ever heard was within a group of seven- to eleven-year-olds from a legacy church. The passion and power in their prayer was extraordinary. They cried out to God, begging Him to save the nation. They laid down their lives before Him, entreating Him to use them. We happen to have this prayer time on a CD, and whenever we play it publicly, the presence of God can be felt in a tangible way. We listen to it frequently at home because it never fails to move and inspire us.

Intercession is an unseen work that involves many hours on one's face before the Lord. Are there people in this movement who will rise to the challenge and make prayer their life call? As God develops fervent and passionate intercessors, He prepares us for the transformation of the nations that we long for. "Unless the Lord builds the house, those who build it labor in vain" (Psalm 127:1, ESV).

A. T. Pierson, a preacher and writer from the turn of the nineteenth century, once said: "From the day of Pentecost, there has been not one great spiritual awakening in any land which has not begun in a union of prayer, though only among two or three. And no such outward, upward movement has continued after such prayer meetings have declined."

And according to John Wesley, "God does nothing except in answer to prayer."

Are we willing to pay the price for an ongoing and sustained move of God?

9

IMAGES OF CHURCH

When we began meeting as a church within the medical school in the 1970s, we decided right from the start that our only textbook on church was going to be the Bible. We set ourselves on a course to study and see what it had to say about the church and church life.

THE BODY OF CHRIST

One of the most frequent pictures we found in the New Testament was that of the church functioning as a body—the body of Christ. Simple church is about being the body of Christ with Christ Himself as the head. The natural body has many different parts, each with its own function. All are necessary for the healthy operation of the body. So it is with the body of Christ.

According to Romans 12 and 1 Corinthians 12, we each have different roles, all of which are necessary for the body to be fit and strong. None of us can manage without the others. If one member is not functioning properly, then the entire body of Christ is weaker because of it.

So we embrace differences and diversity in the body of Christ and welcome the various gifts and ways of functioning of each member. Some people will have more practical skills—we know one person who repairs the cars of those in his church who cannot afford to fix them. Others will be gifted in worship or prophecy. But all of us working together make up the body of Christ.

In 1 Corinthians 12:22-25, Paul takes this idea one step further and says we should give even greater honor to the weaker parts of the body. How does this work itself out in practice? In our experience, it seems that when someone who is naturally quiet makes a comment, his or her insights are usually quite profound. Children are another example. By valuing and applauding their contributions, we can help children grow in their confidence to participate within the body of Christ.

In the West, church is often more of a spectator sport rather than a team event. We sit in the pews and gaze at the back of someone's head when we are supposed to be, as the late John Wimber, who founded the Vineyard movement, put it, "doing the stuff!" Wimber's very practical teaching showed ordinary believers how to "do the stuff" that occupied Jesus and the disciples—healing the sick, casting out demons, praying for emotional needs (Luke 4:18-21). Both 1 Corinthians 14 and Romans 12 list what we could be doing—everything from prophesying and giving to healing and working miracles.

CHURCH AS FAMILY

As our group of medical students studied what the New Testament had to say about church, another metaphor that emerged was that of a family. Simple church is family. The other members are our spiritual brothers, sisters, sons, and daughters. We do not "go to" family—it is not an event or a place. We *are* family. Of course, healthy families do get together—often. But it is not their getting together that makes them family; it is their relationship with one another.

Likewise, it is not the meeting itself that makes a church, but the relationships. Being the body of Christ involves much more than meetings. Christ commanded us to love one another (John 15:12, 17) and said that the world would know us by that love (John 13:35). The early disciples understood this and shared their lives together in deep and meaningful ways. John, who described himself as "the disciple Jesus loved," talked at length in his first letter about the nature of fellowship: "If we walk in the light as He is in the light, we have fellowship with one another" (1 John 1:7).

Wolfgang Simson writes,

House church Christianity is the body of Christ in an ordinary house. . . . In many ways a house church is like a spiritual, extended family, relational, spontaneous and organic. For its everyday life a house church does not need a higher level of organization, bureaucracy and ceremonies than any ordinary large family. The house church reflects God's qualities and character. This community lifestyle is moulded in the spirit of love, truth,

*forgiveness, faith and grace. House churches are the way
we love each other, forgive each other, mourn with those
who mourn and laugh with those who laugh, extend
and receive grace and constantly remain in touch with
God's truth and forgiveness. It is a place where all masks
can fall, and we can be open to each other and still keep
loving each other.*[1]

This is authentic fellowship. It is being real with one another, loving and caring for one another genuinely and without hypocrisy. It is the knowledge that if someone is having difficulties, we know that person well enough to recognize the signs. It is learning to take off the masks that we all wear and allowing people to know us as we really are. True fellowship takes time and commitment.

The apostle John comes to this startling conclusion: "Anyone who does not love his brother, whom he has seen, cannot love God, whom he has not seen" (1 John 4:20, NIV).

Our friend Jared Looney works in New York's inner city. He recently reflected on one of his simple church's meetings:

*This past weekend, the church that meets in our home took
twists and turns that led to a powerful evening of mutual
support and steps taken toward emotional healing. First,
half of our usual participants didn't make it for various
reasons (illness, work-related issues, etc.), and then we had
some visitors from out of town in addition to some of our
summer interns. The gathering quickly became a diverse
community of friends. As we moved toward the end of our
discussion of the Scriptures, a couple of people began to*

share—in raw and honest terms—their current struggles and pain. With tears and frustration, they spoke with authentic candor of their wrestling with God and trust during their own "dark nights of the soul."

These tear-soaked conversations are not at all weekly occurrences in our simple churches; however, they are common. And I was reminded with real clarity why I so eagerly embrace such a simple, messy approach to church. How many fade into the shadows, embittered simply because they needed an unconditional embrace and to open their mouths and speak from their hearts but found no such circle of friends? How many grasp for some remnant of faith as they struggle with the juxtaposition of the choir's song and the emptiness in their own hearts? And how many more actively escape such vulnerability because their consumerism has inoculated them to grace and to the scandal of the Cross?

Our cities are desperate for Good News and for families of believers that make faith and hope tangible. Our city is saturated with disappointment. It covers us like a cloud drenched in cold winter rain. Simply stated, people need something that is real. Real faith. Real love. Real hope. I'm not sure from where it will emerge if not from fellow strugglers finding real courage to live out the Good News in authentic community. Pray for that. Pray for that to multiply over and over again in our city. The barriers to evangelism here are so often our own Western inventions. There are many whose hearts are vulnerable to the Good News, but so few workers. Pray to the Lord of the harvest.[2]

A TEMPLE BUILT WITH LOVING STONES

The New Testament also paints the church as a spiritual temple built with living stones (1 Peter 2:5). These stones have to be cut and chiseled in order to fit together. Living a community lifestyle helps to grind us into shape. As we grow together in our relationships, particularly as this works itself out on a daily basis, tensions occur. Someone doesn't like the way that another person handles the children. Another prefers a different style of music. As we share our lives together, we have many opportunities to learn to die to ourselves and our own preferences. This is God's way of transforming us to be more like Jesus.

The New Testament Christians obviously spent much time together, but how can this be done in the busyness of life today? Often, people feel they can only invite others into their homes if everything is perfect—not a speck of dust on the furniture, the kids all on their best behavior, and a gourmet home-cooked meal sitting on the stove. But if that is our standard, we will never get to know each other! Why not invite another family to join you for pizza before you take the kids to the ball game? Or invite a single mom and her children over to watch a movie?

Colossians 2:19 says that the body is being nourished and knit together by joints and ligaments, growing with the increase that is from God. The words used to describe the joints and ligaments actually mean "bonded together." Love is the glue that bonds us together. This love is practical, not mere warm fuzzies. Sometimes practical love might mean collecting money for a person in financial need. It might involve cleaning the home of someone unable to do it for him- or herself.

When we lived in London, one of our home groups included

several nurses who worked odd shifts. We lived in a tough, inner-city neighborhood, and their only way home was to take public transportation—not particularly pleasant late at night, to say nothing of the safety issues. The members of this home group decided they did not want the nurses using public transportation so late at night. Each week they collected a copy of the nurses' schedules, and someone would meet them with a car whenever they came off duty to make sure they traveled home safely. That was easy for the first week or two. But think of the commitment involved when this went on month after month! That truly was a practical expression of laying down one's life for someone else.

10

SIMPLY REPRODUCIBLE

So what makes simple church different from a typical legacy church? Isn't it just like one of the legacy church's home groups or cell groups?

Simple church is not really like anything else you may have experienced as "church."[1] When people hear about simple church, they are often filled with questions. "Is it like a prayer meeting?" Well, we do pray, but no, it is not like a prayer meeting. "Is it a Bible study?" No, it is not a Bible study, although we will usually spend some time in the Word.

Perhaps the greatest temptation that we believers from traditional churches face when starting a simple church is to make our gatherings a miniature version of what we have always known. We have come across some house churches that set up chairs in rows and have a pulpit! Even when we sit in a more informal circle so we can see each other, it's still easy to slip into the habit of doing traditional church in our home. Someone prepares the worship, another the teaching, and so on. But the only thing we have done is exchange the walls of the church building for those of our living room. If we do that, we miss out on what simple church is all about—the Lord Himself having a plan for our times together and revealing Himself by working through each member of His body.

People may leave a traditional church, but it sometimes takes a long time for the tradition to leave them! Initially they are likely to feel guilty every Sunday morning when they don't go to a service. As Frank Viola suggests in his book *Gathering in Homes*, especially when starting a new church with people who have come out of a legacy church, it may be best to simply share a meal together for a number of weeks without attempting to have any kind of "religious" or "spiritual" meeting. Getting to know one another in a nonreligious context is an important ingredient for allowing the Lord to knit a group of people together relationally and spiritually.[2]

Church is family. When a family gathers around the dinner table, the mother doesn't say to the children, "Now let's all listen to what Dad has to say," before the father talks for forty minutes explaining something of little relevance to the kids. No way! Healthy families are interactive, participatory, and intensely relevant to the people in them. And simple church is the same way.

Every living thing in God's creation is born to reproduce, even church. And the simpler it is, the easier it is to reproduce. Rabbits multiply more rapidly than elephants because of their size and uncomplicated structure. This principle permeates all of life, and church is no exception.

If we hope to see these simple churches multiply, then we need to pay attention to what we model. All of the key elements of simple church are as basic as possible. It's not that the content is simplistic or shallow—it is often very profound—but the pattern for doing it is simple and therefore easily replicated.

Take, for example, prayer. If we model five-minute sermon prayers, we will inhibit all but the most mature Christians from praying out loud. If, on the other hand, we pray simple, two- or three-sentence conversational prayers, anyone is able to join in, and people can pray multiple times.

If we produce a gourmet meal, people will think they have to be expert cooks to start a church in their home. A simple potluck, however, involves the participation of everyone.

If we preach a sermon, others think they have to be able to preach. (Since the greatest fear most people have is fear of public speaking, this is hardly likely to encourage active participation!) But anyone can lead by using simple, interactive methods of Bible study. A Filipino church planter says it this way: "I never do anything in church that a one-week-old Christian would be unable to do." We love that.

Acts 2:42 provides a simple framework for what happened when the early Christians came together. "They devoted themselves to the apostles' teaching and to the fellowship, to the breaking of bread and to prayer" (NIV). These four elements define what happens in simple churches. It is not that all these things have to happen in every gathering or in the same order, but more that the Holy Spirit is likely to lead the group within those parameters.

LEARNING FROM THE BIBLE

Let's look at the apostles' teaching first. If our simple churches are going to multiply rapidly, we no longer have the luxury of taking several years to train a Bible teacher. Anyway, the goal is not a few gifted teachers but a lot of hungry learners. Paul the apostle faced this dilemma as well—in some instances he was forced to move away from the new believers almost immediately. For example, in Philippi he only "stayed there several days" (Acts 16:12, NIV). Therefore, we like to use an approach that allows the Bible to teach itself, enabling even young believers to lead. In New Testament times, teaching was far more interactive. For instance, the word used for Paul's lengthy teaching in Ephesus is the Greek word *dialegomai*, from which we get our word "dialogue" (Acts 20:7). Jesus' informal teaching was frequently discussion-based and interrupted by questions He either posed Himself or was asked by others.

Evangelical Christians tend to emphasize the importance of good *teaching*, but we believe that this is missing the point of helping people to genuinely *learn* Scripture and *apply* it to their everyday lives. Statistics show that we learn far more by actively participating than we do by hearing alone. People remember approximately 20 percent of what they hear, 50 percent of what they see and hear, and 70 percent of what they say themselves.[3] In simple church, everyone is involved in the learning process. More than once, we have had people tell us they have learned more in just a few months of simple church than in years of listening to good sermons!

Over the years, we have come back repeatedly to two or three different patterns of Bible study. The method is not the vital issue, but what is important is that the method leads to a participatory discussion.

The pattern that we use to teach most often is based on four symbols: a question mark, a lightbulb, an arrow, and an ear. We begin with a passage of Scripture, and one person in the group reads aloud a verse or a sentence. Occasionally (for example, with one of the parables or a gospel story), it may be appropriate to read the whole passage before going back to explore it verse by verse. The group then looks for things that correspond to the symbols. The question mark obviously signifies something we don't understand. A person might say, "I have a question mark on this verse. What does it mean when it says . . . ?"

The lightbulb is used to represent something that sheds light, either on that passage of Scripture or something going on in a person's life. So one person in the group might say, "I have a lightbulb on this verse. This describes a situation that happened to me at work last week . . . "

The arrow represents God piercing a person's heart—he or she has heard from God and needs to do something about it. A participant in the group might say, "God has been speaking to me about this for a while, but I've been ignoring it. I'm going to have to change. . . . This is an arrow for me!" Or, "I've just realized from this verse that God wants me to . . ."

The ear represents someone who needs to hear about what a person has just learned. This is usually applied at the end of the study, and there's accountability built in. The next week those gathered can ask, "Did you talk about what you learned last week to somebody during the week?"

Once a verse or thought has been covered, then we move on to the next one.

We have frequently used this method to start churches, especially when working with unbelievers. With our group of not-yet-Christian businesspeople, we studied the book of Proverbs in this fashion, looking at principles relating to business and wealth. Although it began as a business-focused study, over time, every person in the group became a Christian! The seed of the Kingdom is the Word of God, which is living and active and life changing (Luke 8:11; Hebrews 4:12).

Another pattern we use in simple church is to read a verse and then ask everyone to comment on it, answering three questions: What does it say? What does it mean? What difference does it make in my life? We used this pattern with a group of new believers in a low-income housing project. When we came to the 1 Thessalonians 4 teaching on sexual sin, one of the young men who had only been a Christian a few weeks and was still living with his girlfriend asked, "Does this verse mean that the piece of paper is important?" (referring to the marriage license). The group spent most of that week discussing the verse. We did not give the answers but let the Scripture do the teaching instead. The result? The Holy Spirit convicted this young man through the Scriptures and he lived separately from his girlfriend until they were married.

It is also important that people pass on what they are learning to others: "Who do you know who needs to hear what we have just discussed? Share with them about this over the next few days and let us know next week how it went."

Recently Felicity "attended" a Web seminar put on by David Watson. He described how he had taught basic patterns similar to the ones described in this chapter to a simple church he had been working with. He had encouraged them to pass on what they were learning to others. Within a year, a group that started with six people was now involved in ten different simple churches with well over sixty people attending.[4]

Larger groups may run more smoothly if someone acts as a facilitator—to make sure that the study keeps moving, that everyone is taking part, and that no one (particularly the facilitator) dominates. It is not the facilitator's job to answer questions but rather to direct the questions back to the group: "What does anyone else think about this question?" "Have we studied anything else that relates to this topic?" By continually pointing people back to the Scriptures, the facilitator ensures that the Bible remains the authority.

In this type of participatory Bible study, everyone's opinions are valued and there is no such thing as a wrong answer. When someone shares something bizarre, the facilitator might say, "That's an interesting point. I've never heard anyone express it that way before. What does anyone else think?" Someone is bound to come up with a better answer. If you imply that what that person said was wrong, he or she may never share again.

Many who come from traditional church backgrounds are concerned that such an approach opens the door to heresy. We can attest that in the dozens of groups we've been part of over the years, we have never seen anyone sidetracked by wrong teaching. Even with the youngest Christians, we've found that when anything too outlandish comes up someone will usually point it out.

In the churches we've been involved with, we usually study a book of the Bible. Sometimes we cover as much as a whole chapter in a session; more frequently, however, it's just a few verses. Because literacy may be a problem in some groups, we usually read only a couple of verses before stopping to discuss what we are learning. Even if the adults are unable to read (or have forgotten their glasses again!), there will usually be a child around who can read the verses.

The method you choose to use is not as important as accomplishing your goal of creating a participatory Bible study. The Bible itself is the teacher, and everyone in the group is involved in both the teaching and learning, as well as applying what is learned to daily life.

While this does not necessarily mean there is no place for teaching by a gifted teacher, we've found that small meetings in homes are not the best setting for extended, lesson-type messages. If God has revealed some helpful or exciting truth to someone, we always encourage that person to share it—but in a brief form. The hard fact is that listening to long discourses does not turn people into disciples!

In fact, research conducted by The Barna Group has revealed that in conventional churches across the United States, within two hours of having left a church service, the typical attender cannot identify the topic of the sermon, much less the key points communicated within it! While there are many people who appreciate well-crafted and flawlessly communicated sermons, there are even more who appear to get little value from them. Yet these are people who chose to attend the church service because of their desire to connect more deeply with God— they are not closed to learning and worshiping. We simply need to offer them options that are more appropriate for their style of growth.

FOOD AND FELLOWSHIP

The next two elements of the Acts 2:42 framework are fellowship and eating together.

We have been involved in simple church meetings now for most of the last thirty years and have come to believe that meals are very important in determining whether a group will be successful or not. Groups that eat together invariably seem to do better than those that do not.

The meal is a great time for fellowship and sharing our lives together. It's a time to ask questions of those in our group: What has gone well for you in the last few days? How has God spoken to you? What have you been learning from the Word? Where are you struggling? Eating together offers a chance for people to be transparent, to let down the masks and get real with each other.

Eating obviously played an important part in Jesus' life as well. Some of His most effective interactions with believers and unbelievers alike occurred over a meal, including His meal with Matthew (Levi) and his friends (Mark 2:15) and the Last Supper (Matthew 26:26). In Acts 2:46, we learn that the early church shared meals daily with great joy, and 1 Corinthians 11 tells of the problems that arose when some people failed to share the common meal (a time for remembering the Lord's death) appropriately.

While eating together is important, we have found some guidelines and patterns to be helpful. In general, our meals are simple potlucks in which everyone brings a dish. If the group is meeting in the evening, it is easy for those who are working to pick up something from a store on their way to the meeting.

If our group includes families who are struggling to make ends meet, we send the leftovers home with them, a sensitive way of helping them out. (We sometimes even cook extra food so that we know there will be plenty for people to take home.) Our occasional celebrations, when all of the local home churches come together, also include a potluck meal, as do the times when the leaders of simple churches or networks of churches get together.

A meal is also a very natural way to share Communion. This symbolic part of the meal—a sharing together of bread and wine—does not need to be any more of a ritual than other aspects of our times together. There is nothing in the Scriptures that indicates that it needs to be served by someone with special training or done in a particularly solemn or formal fashion. We encourage Communion as a time of focused reflection on what the Lord has done for us. Sometimes we do this by asking everyone to take a piece of bread from a loaf on the table and then share it with several others while praying for them. A family might gather to share this together, or maybe a group of friends will pull in a visitor to include him or her in this representation of Christ's death on the cross.

PRAYER

Prayer is the fourth element simple churches incorporate from Acts 2:42. We sometimes ask a person requesting prayer to sit on the "hot seat" while others lay hands on that person and pray for the need. Someone might share prophetic words or pictures, and someone else might share a verse of Scripture. We've found this kind of prayer to be life changing!

At other times, we break the groups of ten or twenty into

smaller groups of three to four for prayer. In this way, we make sure that everyone in the group can easily take an active part in the praying.

Again, we've found Vineyard founder John Wimber's teaching to be helpful in this area. He taught that faith is spelled R-I-S-K. It can be a risk to boldly pray for specific answers, but we've found that God wonderfully responds when we step out in faith.

Simple, basic patterns of the four elements found in Acts 2:42 can be learned by anyone. Believers just a few days old in the Lord can apply these patterns to lead a group of their friends in learning from the Bible and having fellowship together. In this way, small and simple churches can multiply quickly.

11

MARCHING TO THE SPIRIT'S DRUMBEAT

WHEN WE WERE still in our medical school church, sometimes our times together were painful; it seemed that the Lord was not in attendance with us at all. There were long periods of silence, not because we were lost in His presence, but because we were just hoping that someone would do or say something! Sometimes it was so bad that we all just went home. But gradually over the months, the presence of the Lord became more and more of a reality in the meetings. We learned the value of being led by the Holy Spirit, and we frequently experienced the Holy Spirit orchestrating the meeting in extraordinary ways.

Sometimes the presence of the Lord was so real that we would spend the whole time in worship. We can remember a period of time when we were going through the book of

Nehemiah. One week, we came to what should have been a very boring passage; it was a list of the different people who were responsible for rebuilding various sectors of the walls of Jerusalem. It would have been very natural to gloss over that section and get to something more stimulating or relevant. But somehow the Holy Spirit illumined the passage, and as one after another person shared, a mounting excitement could be felt in the room because God was speaking to us. Through that passage, the Holy Spirit taught us the critical need for each person to take his or her part in the body of Christ. And He did so in a way that was so memorable we can still recall it many years later!

What we learned during those years formed the foundation of what we now do when we get together. The passage most relevant to understanding our times together is 1 Corinthians 14:26: "Whenever you come together, each of you has a psalm, has a teaching, has a tongue, has a revelation, has an interpretation. Let all things be done for edification."

When we moved to the United States and finally began a simple church, we determined from the start that we would live out this verse. People would not sit as spectators in meetings, but all would be actively drawn in. For the first two years, none of the people in the church saw or heard a "sermon." Everything, including any teaching, was done in a highly interactive fashion. Sometimes it was next to impossible to figure out who was leading in a meeting. But this was okay. What mattered was that Jesus was seen as the center of the gathering.

We believe that one of the most important concepts of the Kingdom is that of the priesthood of all believers (1 Peter 2:9). We are all important, and one of the benefits of simple church is that our gatherings are open times when everyone can bring what is on his or her heart. A typical gathering (is there such a thing?) will involve a meal; it might also include worship—singing, reading Scriptures, praise—then maybe a prophecy or picture/vision that the Holy Spirit gives to someone. This might lead us in a variety of directions: in-depth discussion, ministry to the needs of those in the group, sharing what we have been learning throughout the week, or praying for an area of the city where we want to start a new church—the possibilities are endless. Sometimes this will all happen around the meal table. Other times it will occur once people have finished eating and are sitting informally in the living area. In every part of our times together we are learning to follow the Holy Spirit.

Following the Holy Spirit in this type of open meeting often begins with each of us bringing what the Lord is teaching us, letting spiritual gifts flow, and encouraging everyone to pray for and open up to each other. It is not by chance that teaching on the nature of Christian gatherings in 1 Corinthians 11–14 includes the famous verses about the gifts of the Holy Spirit in chapter 12, and also puts them into a workable context by explaining that everything needs to be bathed in love in chapter 13!

Following the Holy Spirit in our times together is an adventure, and we've found that there is no limit to what the Lord might do! He knows what is going on in our lives, and if we let Him, He will touch and change us and the world around us. Our time together is never boring when it is led by the Holy Spirit.

Sometimes people wonder how the Holy Spirit leads in a time together. We've found that if we fully participate in what is going on, the things that come to mind spontaneously are most likely from the Holy Spirit. For example, if someone is praising God through prayer, you might find that a verse of Scripture or a song comes to mind. Chances are, that thought was the Holy Spirit, and it's something you should share with the group. You are always seeking to follow the thread that the Holy Spirit is weaving.

If we are learning to hear God's voice in our ordinary, every-day lives, then we will also become familiar with hearing His voice in our time together. After all, His sheep hear His voice (John 10:3-4).

Since God is creative, we've come to expect variety in our meetings: gifts of the Spirit such as prophecy, prayer, scriptural insights, and visions. And we've learned not to be concerned about making mistakes. In a sense, each gathering is a work-shop, and the best way to learn is to risk making mistakes.

You may be wondering if it's necessary to be "charismatic" in order to have simple church. (By charismatic we mean those who have had an experience of "being filled or baptized with the Holy Spirit," usually subsequent to conversion. Often people with this experience use the gifts of the Spirit that are described in 1 Corinthians 12.) Simple churches, like evangelical churches of other types, take a variety of theological positions on this subject. But usually, it is a nonissue. Not only that, some of the most Spirit-led people we know would not claim to have had any kind of charismatic experience. Often we have heard them using gifts of the Spirit, even if they would not call them that. For example, a charismatic person might talk about "prophecy," while someone without this experience might say, "I think God is saying . . ." or "Something has come to mind . . ." In our experience, God seems to be blurring the distinctions more and more between charismatic and noncharismatic believers. Our own experience is that God delights to fill His people with His Spirit and to give them spiritual (supernatural) gifts that are frequently used, not just when we get together, but also in ordinary, day-to-day life.

If you are facilitating a meeting, you might begin by asking people to share what God is doing in their lives. This invitation can act as a springboard for people to share a song or a Scripture the Holy Spirit has put on their hearts. As the gathering continues, watch for and focus on the things that the Holy Spirit is doing. For example, if someone shares a need, the Lord probably wants to minister to that need. The facilitator might ask people, "What do you think the Lord wants us to do about this?" Someone may suggest, "Let's gather around her and pray." If someone shares a praise report, someone else might have a song on his heart that expresses praise to God. In general, unless something goes against the flow of what is happening, you can view it as the activity of the Holy Spirit. Encourage people to participate in ways that fit in with what is already going on. A theme often emerges, and all can see the Lord is speaking clearly.

Once we open ourselves to Jesus' presence, He shares His heart with us, and as we listen to Him, He draws us closer to Himself and leads us in the direction He has planned for us. It is as though we are the instruments in an orchestra, each with our own distinctive tone. The Holy Spirit is the conductor, and as we play the melody He has given us individually, He produces a symphony.

This pattern of waiting on God cannot be organized and

planned. It cannot be made into a program. It is spontaneous and natural, and it brings life.

Let us describe one of our favorite meetings—not typical, perhaps, but attention grabbing. This occurred in a new church that had started in one of the less affluent areas of town—with new believers straight out of the harvest.

Maybe twenty of us were gathered in a tiny apartment—up the stairs, in the kitchen, all over the living room. We had just finished the meal; the leftover food and dishes were being cleared. All of a sudden we heard a commotion outside—raised voices and cursing. One of the adults went out to check on the situation and found that two of the kids had had a disagreement and gotten into a fistfight. The "offender" was hauled off to a bedroom, but two of his relatives then disagreed on what to do with him. When things had calmed down and the other kids were settled outside with some helpers, the adults sat down. The atmosphere was, to say the least, a little strained!

"What do you do when you hate someone?" One of the new believers most closely involved in the situation blurted out this heartfelt question. Was this the Holy Spirit leading us to study this subject? You bet! So we spent some time looking in the Bible at ways a Christian handles hatred, what we do when we disagree, and some of the principles for bringing up children. After a fruitful hour of discussion, with many stories from others of how Jesus had helped them in these areas, we moved into prayer. Obviously we prayed about the things that had come up during the discussion. Was this the Holy Spirit again? Of course! We gathered around those who wanted prayer. All of us (not just the "mature" believers) prayed with each person individually, laying hands on them and asking the

Lord to help them in these areas of their lives. The atmosphere was infused with the presence of Jesus. The Holy Spirit was at work in our lives.

We then invited the eight or ten kids back inside. They loved to sing and worship and all had a favorite song or two. It was loud and out of tune, but very genuine and real. At one point Felicity opened her eyes as we were singing "Shout to the Lord" and saw that two boys about eight or nine years old were singing their hearts out, eyes closed, heads raised.

It may have been messy, but we somehow suspect the Lord was more pleased with this simple expression of His body than with our professional performances or staged shows.

12

THE GREAT OMISSION

MILLIONS ARE CURRENTLY moving into simple churches. But the present reality here in the West is that this growth is primarily being driven by Christians transferring from traditional to simple churches. There are notable exceptions to this, of course, but we cannot yet describe what is happening here as substantial net growth in the Kingdom of God. We do believe, however, that through this, God is preparing and equipping ordinary people to bring in a great harvest. Indeed, there are already signs that this is beginning to occur. We are hearing story after story of ordinary believers going outside the four walls of their simple churches to work with groups of not-yet-believers and disciple them to faith in Christ. A friend of ours, for example, sets aside one day a week for evangelism. During the morning he prays and asks the Lord where he should go that day to find someone to speak to about Jesus. He commits himself to responding to what he senses the Lord telling him to do. On one occasion, in a store owned by Moslems, he found himself kneeling on their prayer mat and asking God to bless this family and business. The family was overjoyed to receive this blessing.

It is interesting to note that Jesus never actually told His followers to plant churches. In what has become known as the great commission, He told us to make disciples:

> *All authority has been given to Me in heaven and on earth. Go therefore and make disciples of all the nations, baptizing them in the name of the Father and of the Son and of the Holy Spirit, teaching them to observe all things that I have commanded you; and lo, I am with you always, even to the end of the age.*
> —MATTHEW 28:18-20

As we go to where it is spiritually dark, the light and fragrance of Jesus will permeate the place. As we impact pockets of lost people and make disciples, Jesus builds His church.

In our Western culture, however, it is easy for the great commission to become the great omission. According to David Barrett and Todd Johnson in *World Christian Trends*, the total cost of Christian outreach worldwide averages $330,000 for each newly baptized person. The cost per baptism in the United States tops $1.5 million.[1] (This figure reflects the expenses of church buildings, staff, seminary training, and so on.) Tragically the average Protestant church sees only one or two come to

Christ a year. Since we all know of churches that see hundreds responding to Jesus each year, this means that, actually, the average Protestant church probably sees no converts in any given year! What has happened?

In nations where there is substantial net gain for the Kingdom, one of the characteristics of church planting is a commitment to evangelism. In many countries of the world, people pay a high price to preach the gospel. Some are beaten, some are thrown into prison, and some even lose their lives. Yet they count it a privilege to suffer for the sake of the gospel (Acts 5:41). Our Western Christianity appears anemic in comparison.

Acts 8 tells us that after Stephen's death, a great persecution arose against the church and they were all scattered. It goes on, "Therefore those who were scattered went everywhere preaching the word" (Acts 8:4). If we want to be part of a rapidly growing church planting movement, we must be willing to have our lives affected and inconvenienced by following Jesus into the harvest. Without abundant and purposeful evangelism, we are unlikely to see the magnitude of growth for which we long, the kind of growth that has become the norm in other parts of the world. The principle holds true: If we sow sparingly we will reap sparingly, but if we sow bountifully we will reap bountifully (2 Corinthians 9:6).

We desire a church that is easily accessible—not just geographically but also culturally and socially—to every person in every city and every nation. We want to see expressions of the body of Christ in every neighborhood, apartment complex, retirement center, school, college dormitory, and office building. But this also needs to be a *relevant* expression of Jesus' family in every people grouping and subculture. How is this going to come about?

In Mark 1:17, Jesus called two commercial fishermen, Peter and Andrew, to follow Him: "Follow Me, and I will make you become fishers of men." As we follow Jesus, He will teach us how to effectively reach out to the lost.

GO

Matthew 28:18 starts by declaring that all authority belongs to Jesus. He has authority over demons and diseases. And He gives to His disciples that same authority so we can see people healed and set free in His name (Matthew 10:1). We are not talking about a powerless gospel here.

The great commission says, "Go" (or perhaps more accurately, "Having gone") make disciples. Yet rather than going, we ask people to come! Come to church; come to our special meeting. Biblically, we are the ones who, as we go out into the marketplace, take the Kingdom with us.

If we ask not-yet-believers to come to our church, we ask them to do something that feels very foreign to them. We expect them to sing songs they don't know, listen to a monologue about concepts they probably don't understand, and give their lives to a person they don't yet believe in. Praise God that some people do become followers of Jesus in such a situation. But Jesus always sent His disciples out to the people (Luke 9:2; 10:3). When we *go*, rather than asking people to come, we are the ones to take the first step in getting out of our comfort zones and crossing cultural barriers.

Paul understood this: "I have become all things to all men, that I might by all means save some" (1 Corinthians 9:22).

Sadly, many Christians do not have friends who are unbelievers. They live in Christian ghettos of their own making; all of their "real" friends are church friends. They are afraid to mix with "outsiders" for fear of being contaminated by their sin or out of concern their own faith will not be strong enough to withstand temptation. But if we do not go into places where "sinners" hang out, how are we going to reach them? As our friend Neil Cole[2] likes to say, "Christians have to learn to sit in the smoking section."

Recent studies bear out the fact that most followers of Christ are not focused on diverting their friends into the Kingdom of God. A national study by The Barna Group among born-again Christians found that only one out of every five has nurtured a friendship with a non-Christian in the hope of having an opportunity to share their faith in Christ with that person.

Jesus Himself was often called a "friend of sinners" (Matthew 11:19), hanging out with "disreputable sinners" (Matthew 9:10; Mark 2:15-16, NLT). Jesus did not flinch when a prostitute washed His feet with her tears and dried them with her hair (Luke 7:36-50). The only people Jesus seemed uncomfortable with were the Pharisees—the upright, Bible-believing churchgoers of His day.

There are many different ways to get involved with those who don't yet know Jesus. It's simply a matter of making others your priority. You might begin by joining a club or local organization that is devoted to a common interest (see http://www.meetup.com). If you are a parent, get to know your children's friends and their parents. Ask Jesus and He will show you a way. Neil Cole tells the story of a time in Long Beach when he and his team planned to start a coffeehouse. They thought this would be a great way to meet new people, but while he was praying over this, Neil felt the Lord say to him, *Why are you thinking about starting a coffeehouse when there are already many great coffeehouses in this area where the people who don't know Me are congregating?* Neil and his team started hanging out at a local coffeehouse where many people who practiced satanism and witchcraft met. Within months, he formed strong relationships with the people there and soon these people were coming to Jesus.

MAKE DISCIPLES

The great commission tells us to make disciples, which is far more than a "decision" or "prayer of salvation." God wants disciples, not mere converts. He is seeking a radical life change, a whole new way of living. Too often, we are content when someone prays the "sinner's prayer." But Jesus says that new converts who love Him will keep His commandments (John 14:15). True repentance means turning one's life around so that it bears the fruit of a transformed life.

REACH THE NATIONS

The great commission tells us to make disciples of nations, but we have little concept of what it really means to bring a nation to the Lord. We get excited if we see one individual come to Christ! What is a nation? The Greek word used in this passage is *ethne*, from which we get our word *ethnic*. It carries the connotations of a group of people with a distinctive culture—their own customs, language, and way of looking at the world. This obviously includes different nationalities, but it would also include other types of social grouping. Take, for example, skate-boarders. They have their own dress, vocabulary, and lifestyle that an outsider would not fit into. Any city has a multitude of such groups—mall rats (teenagers who hang out in shopping malls), artists, those in low-income housing projects, and so on. The list is endless. In our own city only the middle-class white families (and maybe the Chinese) have enough churches to represent their culture. The others are basically unreached. For example, 50 percent of our city lives in multiunit housing, and 95 percent of them are unchurched.

A survey conducted at the University of Texas in Austin identified around five hundred different subgroups of students on the campus. Examples of these groups include students involved in the arts who live in a certain dorm, and PhD engineering students from India. The survey was conducted for Campus Renewal Ministries, an organization that operates in many universities across the nation to help the different ministries on campus work cooperatively together. Campus Renewal trains students to start "missional communities" in each of these subgroupings, with the goal of creating a missional community for every identified subgroup. By the end of 2008, they had more than 200 of these groups within the University of Texas.

How can we tell when a nation is discipled? By identifying when that people group or subculture has multiplying churches with indigenous (local) leaders needing little or no outside help.

The book of Acts records very few examples of individuals becoming believers. Usually a whole household was involved (Acts 10:24; 16:15). We personally find it easier to work with a group, whether it is a family or a group of friends. Often the whole group will become disciples together, and it is much easier to form a community (i.e., a simple church) where strong relationships already exist than it is to add people one by one to a group and expect them to share their lives together. It is also easier to reach out along relational lines. In some of the churches we started with our kids' friends, we saw the group as a whole come to faith.

BAPTIZE

The great commission also tells us to baptize new believers. In the New Testament, people were baptized on the same day they repented and committed their lives to the Lord. On the Day of Pentecost, three thousand new followers of Jesus were baptized immediately (Acts 2:41). We believe this is an important point. George Patterson, a missionary statesman, believes that a delay in baptism results in slowing down or even killing a movement of rapidly multiplying churches. Occasionally there may be reasons to delay baptism, such as sickness, or in certain cultures, waiting for other family members to become believers. The important thing is that baptism is not seen as something that has to be earned (by going through a new-believers course or living the "right" lifestyle for a year) and that it happens as soon as possible. We believe that baptism is far more than a person just witnessing to friends. It is a "rite of passage" from the kingdom of darkness to the Kingdom of light. It is the first step into a lifetime of obedience to Jesus' commandments. Something of eternal significance happens in heavenly places when a person is baptized.

According to the great commission, the person who makes the disciple should baptize that new believer. They don't have to find a special baptismal pool. The Ethiopian eunuch said,

"Look! Water! What prevents me from being baptized?" (Acts 8:36). We have baptized people in our hot tub and even the bathtub!

It is interesting to see how other cultures react when someone is baptized. It is not unusual for families of other religious backgrounds to have little or no opposition to someone becoming a Christian. But if that person follows this up by announcing his or her plan to be baptized, often the family becomes very upset. Clearly, Satan understands the significance of baptism and fears the new disciple who is going to actively obey all that Jesus has commanded.

TEACH OBEDIENCE

The great commission instructs us to teach new disciples to know right from the start that as soon as they understand what Jesus wants (whether from the written Word or from hearing the voice of the Lord in their hearts), they are to do it. This will give them a foundation in their walk with the Lord upon which they can build the rest of their lives.

George Patterson says that all the instructions of Jesus fit within seven basic commands:[3]

- repent, believe, and receive the Holy Spirit
- be baptized
- love God and one another, your neighbors, and your enemies
- break bread
- pray in Jesus' name
- give
- make disciples

Active disciples make more disciples. And so the whole cycle repeats (see John 20:21 and 2 Timothy 2:2).

The great commission was not an optional extra for the early disciples. It is time for us to move out from our Christian safe havens too. As it says in Romans 10:14, NLT, "How can they hear about him unless someone tells them?" Not all of us are evangelists, but we can all be witnesses to what He has done in our lives (Acts 1:8). We have the life of Jesus within, and if we ask the Lord for the opportunity to share that life with others, He delights to answer that prayer.

There are many different ways to get started in the disciple-making process. The following are some ideas from our own experiences.

- Draw together people from your circle of influence: We've already talked about our group of business associates. This group started when we asked about a dozen coworkers to join us in a study of business principles while enjoying pizza in our home. Although none of them were active Christians, and most had no experience of church, we used the book of Proverbs as our textbook. These people formed the nucleus of our original church.
- Focus on your children and their friends, and then include the parents. We have followed a similar pattern with a group of older teens and twentysomethings.
- Look within your neighborhood. A couple in one of the home churches we were involved with invited a number of families who lived in their neighborhood to join them for church in their home. Because this couple had already formed friendships with their neighbors, many

of them were willing to come. Not many were Christians at first, but they stayed because of the warmth of the fellowship and the sense of belonging they felt in this couple's home.

- Include the elderly or those living in institutional settings. Felicity once approached the director of activities of a local assisted-living retirement center and asked if she could hold a Bible study for the residents. (The term *church* might have been too threatening here.) The director jumped at the idea, advertised it, prepared the room, and was very encouraging. The residents loved it too, and became involved in leading and participating in the group.
- Reach out at work. A friend of ours who was a new believer asked his employer for permission to use a room at work for prayer and Bible study. Others soon joined him.
- Look for ways to expand and form new churches. We learned early on not to automatically assimilate new attendees into our existing group. One couple came to our meeting for just a couple of weeks before sensing that they could start something in their home and with their contacts. They had around ten non-Christian adults and a dozen kids at their first gathering!
- Consider starting a simple church alongside a mainstream congregation. A family who were committed members of a major liturgical denomination felt they needed to reach out to others of their denomination who were not attending church but still wanted to see their faith come alive.

They met midweek while continuing to support their local congregation on Sundays.

In all these examples, we worked primarily with not-yet-Christians or the unchurched. There are plenty of people out there who are looking for something like this. We do not need to persuade our friends who are content in their more traditional churches to join us.

Anyone can participate in this kind of disciple making. Everyone can reach out to his or her friends. This is an essential part of the DNA of simple church. Some people will be gifted to start churches, and they will probably move on to start other churches, leaving the first one in capable hands. There is no reason why a person should not be involved in more than one church plant at a time. At one stage we were involved in half a dozen new groups simultaneously.

God is also working in encouraging ways in other nations. When we were in India, many people—from pastors and evangelists to new believers, from teenage girls to elderly men, from people with PhDs to people who could not read—shared their experiences with church planting. Some had already planted several churches. The common thread and distinguishing mark of all those who were involved in this movement was not that they had great knowledge, but rather that they had a great love for Jesus and the people around them.

Shanti was a priestess to her fishing village community, serving the goddess of wealth. From an early age she tried to serve her gods by spending hours in worship at the local shrines, where she was revered for her spirituality. One day her brother, a recent Christian convert, gave her a picture of the Holy Spirit descending as a dove on Jesus at His baptism. Shanti added this picture to her shrine of idols and began to worship the picture along with her other gods.

A few days later, while she was worshiping the picture, a bright light filled the room. For hours she was lost in the presence of the living God. Her life changed as she realized that Jesus was the one she was looking for. She shared this with her brother, who explained to her how to become a Christian through the saving work of Christ.

When Shanti renounced her idols, she was beaten by the local Hindu priests; her husband threw her out of the house. Destitute and homeless, she survived by begging for six years, giving much time to prayer and fasting whenever there was no food.

After six years, God challenged Shanti to feed at least ten people a day, even though she was just a beggar herself. From this inauspicious start, right in the village where she had been thrown out of the local temple, she began to build up a congregation of people willing to follow Jesus. When we met Shanti, that number had grown to two hundred. Today, a band of about fifty young people go out with her every week to the surrounding villages and share their testimonies of what Jesus is doing in their lives.

Within two weeks of the conference where we shared, Shanti's group had started half a dozen new churches. Wow! What's our excuse?

13

LUKE 10 PRINCIPLES

UNTIL RECENTLY, the extraordinary growth of simple churches in the United States has been primarily among those who were already believers. However, many of these believers are now reaching out into their communities and circles of influence. Soon, we believe we will begin to see what we all long for—a true multiplication of new disciples for the Kingdom of God.

Take, for example, a recent story from our friend Jared Looney in New York:

Some days ago, I was sitting in McDonald's on the west side of the Bronx where I meet with a small group of teenagers to hang out and discuss faith in Christ. We quickly got into a deep and focused discussion ranging from atonement to sexuality to discipleship to church to baptism and so on. Everyone was involved, thinking and asking questions. At one point, one of the guys said, "I believe in God, but I don't like going to church." His body language put an exclamation point on the statement. It struck me as ironic since he shows up for our neighborhood Bible study nearly every Thursday. One of the other teens recognized the irony and quickly responded, "What do you think this is?"

I chimed in and explained that church doesn't have to be sitting in rows and enduring a sermon, but I also pointed out that we weren't calling our meeting in McDonald's "church" (yet)—mostly because they haven't yet committed their lives to Christ. According to my logic, you need a few committed Christ-followers for something to begin crossing the threshold into becoming a "church."[1]

Several years ago, the International Mission Board of the Southern Baptist Convention noticed a new trend. A growing number of missionaries on the field were reporting stories of churches multiplying in unprecedented numbers. They gave the name "church planting movement" to this phenomenon. They defined a church planting movement as "a rapid and multiplicative increase of indigenous churches planting churches within a given people group or population segment."[2]

When they investigated further, they found that each of these reports shared a similar thread: the majority of the growth seemed to be through new believers. They also researched to see if these movements shared any common characteristics and discovered ten principles, including prayer, abundant gospel sowing, and the fact that the churches met mainly in homes and were led by laypeople.[3]

Over the years we have had the privilege of meeting with a number of those involved in the leadership of church planting movements. Several of them have shared with us that the main passage of Scripture from which they derive their missional principles is Luke 10.

In Luke 10, Jesus provides us with an example of crossing cultures in order to give people the Good News. We believe these are perhaps the most exciting principles involved in releasing church planting movements all over the world. As people are applying these principles in the West, not by following a technique but by responding to the truth the Holy Spirit is bringing out of these Scriptures, they too are seeing disciples made and churches started.[4]

Let's unpack the first few verses of Luke 10 to see what is involved.

TRUST GOD TO PROVIDE THE STRATEGY AND THE WORKERS

The Lord now chose seventy-two other disciples and sent them ahead in pairs to all the towns and places he planned to visit.

—LUKE 10:1, NLT

Jesus had a strategy for the region—just as He has a plan for your area. The disciples' job was to obey His instructions. As you expectantly listen to Him, He will tell you where to go.

Your job is simply to respond to Him. He told His disciples that He was sending them to places He planned to visit. If Jesus sends you somewhere, you can have confidence that He will accompany you. Note that part of the strategy in Luke 10 involves sending the disciples out in pairs rather than as individuals or in large teams.

Christians often complain that their city or neighborhood is difficult to reach. But Jesus says the problem is not the harvest; the harvest is ready now.

> *These were his instructions to them: "The harvest is great, but the workers are few. So pray to the Lord who is in charge of the harvest; ask him to send more workers into his fields."*
> —LUKE 10:2, NLT

Jesus clearly defined the problem as being the lack of laborers. In this passage, we see that Jesus had sent thirty-six church planting teams out, and that was still not enough. His answer to the problem was to pray for more workers. In the same way, we can pray that God sends out laborers into the harvest today.

Sometimes we believe that we need to do things in a particular order: first, we start our simple church; then we get to know each other; and then, when we have matured as a group, we can go out into the harvest.[5] But in reality, these things can and should all happen simultaneously. It's not necessary to wait until we are adequately prepared. Jesus tells us to go now:

> *Do you not say, "There are still four months and then comes the harvest"? Behold, I say to you, lift up your*

eyes and look at the fields, for they are already white
for harvest!
—JOHN 4:35

The word used in Luke 10:2 for "send" actually has an element of violence to it. It is the same word used for casting out demons. We are to cry out to God, pleading with Him to literally thrust out workers into the harvest.

There is another, more subtle point here that we'll clarify later in this chapter when we look at Luke 10:5-6. The disciples were praying for more laborers, but they were not just praying for other church planters like themselves, they were also praying for a "person of peace" who was going to become the laborer in that field. The key person, the "person of peace," for reaching this new group may not even be a Christian yet!

Back in 2002, John White and Kenny Moore were discussing ways to start a church planting movement in their state. As they explored this subject, they realized that Jesus had already given the key in Luke 10:2, so they decided to conduct an experiment. Each day they would pray the prayer of this passage together over the telephone. When they weren't able to connect by phone, they agreed to leave a "voice mail prayer."

Just like the widow in Luke 18, John and Kenny were persistent and specific in their request that God send out laborers into His harvest. And as their praying continued, they started to see things happen. Within his denomination, Kenny was responsible for church planting in his state. Before he and John started praying together, he received an average of one contact a month regarding church planting. But after they began praying, the contacts became an almost daily occurrence. And over a recent eight-month period, Kenny saw more than one hundred simple churches start, as well as twenty more traditional ones. He now claims that prayer like this is his only strategy for church planting.

Kenny and John call this prayer the "10:2b virus," and they are seeking to infect everyone they meet with these concepts. Across the nation, people are partnering to pray the 10:2b prayer daily over the phone. Why not become part of this epidemic?[6]

If you aren't seeing an abundant harvest, you may be looking in the wrong places. According to Jesus, it is the sick who need a physician (Matthew 9:12). You'll be more likely to find receptive people in the trenches and the gutters of life than in pleasant, middle-class, suburban neighborhoods. It is easier to reach out to people who know they have a need and are already seeking answers.

In many church planting movements, a key part of the church planters' strategy is prayer walking. Often they walk the streets of the area where they sense Jesus sending them, praying for the people who live there. They pray blessing on those people and on the city and its services (like the police department, education system, and so on). They repent for the sins of the area. They identify the problems of the area and pray against the spiritual powers of darkness behind them. Prayer like this will open up an area for the gospel.

A friend of ours in India decided to test prayer walking. He adopted two villages in which to plant churches. In one village he prayer walked, and in the other he deliberately did not. After a few months, forty-five new families had come to Christ in the village where he prayer walked. He was chased out of the other village!

TRUST IN GOD'S PROTECTION

Now go, and remember that I am sending you out as
lambs among wolves.

—LUKE 10:3, NLT

Sheep do not possess any natural means of protection. Their only safeguard is their shepherd. Your protection when you go out is Jesus, your Shepherd. We faced this situation in a very real way a few years ago when our daughter, Becky, asked if we would allow her to work in the club and bar district in our city.

"I really sense this is what the Lord wants me to do," she said. Our immediate reaction was fear for Becky's safety. This was followed by an equally poignant question, "What will other Christians think?" We had to trust Jesus to protect her, and we decided that since Jesus was a friend of sinners, it didn't matter what others thought. We learned that when we trust God, He blesses our efforts. Within just a few months, several of those Becky worked with became believers.

In Luke 10:17-19, when the disciples reported back on this assignment, they were excited because even the demons obeyed when they used the name of Jesus. When you go out, you are likely to confront demonic powers. This makes it even more important that Jesus is your protection. In Luke 11:21-22, Jesus tells us to bind the strong man and plunder his goods. The strong man is the devil, and his goods are the people he is holding in captivity. As we do spiritual warfare, we rescue people from the kingdom of darkness.

There's another lesson to be learned in this illustration of sheep. Vulnerability about your weaknesses is actually attractive to others because it will make it easier for people to relate to you.

TRUST GOD TO PROVIDE THE RESOURCES

*Don't take any money with you, nor a traveler's bag, nor
an extra pair of sandals. And don't stop to greet anyone on
the road.*
—LUKE 10:4, NLT

There are a number of reasons for this: First, the resources are actually in the harvest; your provision comes from the people you are going to reach. It is not necessary—or biblical—to go to a new place or group with all it takes to start a church. In order to allow for a spontaneous movement of God, trust Him to provide all that you need, including new leadership, from within the harvest itself. Second, by going without resources, you learn to trust Jesus for your every provision.

Our church planter friends from India will tell you there is yet another reason for going without resources: they don't plan to stay. They realize that they are not the permanent workers in any harvest field. God always provides a local person to take that role—the person of peace, as we will see in the next verses.

We've sometimes made the mistake of staying too long with one group which allows the new church to become dependent on us and makes it much more difficult to transfer leadership to a local person. Staying too long in one place also limits the number of churches we can start. It is much better to hand over leadership to a local person quickly and then continue to disciple that person for as long as necessary. The job of the church planter is then to mentor the new indigenous leader, working closely with him or her outside of the meeting times.

Jesus even goes so far in this verse as to tell us not to stop to greet anyone on the road. This is good advice, especially if you find yourself working in a hostile environment. If you keep your eyes focused on the task, you will be much less likely to stir up opposition by speaking to the wrong people.

TRUST GOD TO LEAD YOU TO THE "PERSON OF PEACE"

Whenever you enter someone's home, first say, "May God's peace be on this house." If those who live there are peaceful, the blessing will stand; if they are not, the blessing will return to you.

—LUKE 10:5-6, NLT

In this passage, Jesus tells us to look for a person of peace and bless that person. You will recognize the person of peace because you will be invited into that person's home or sphere of influence. When you enter, you are to give it your blessing. Note that you are to bless, not curse. Christians often tend to express their disapproval of people rather than finding ways to bless them.

Robbi Sluder found a powerful way to bless and not curse. One Easter Saturday evening as she was preparing her daughter's Easter dress, she was listening to some Christian music. The song was written from Mary Magdalene's perspective as she encountered Jesus after the Resurrection. Suddenly Robbi realized that the first person Jesus chose to reveal Himself to after His resurrection was probably formerly a prostitute. Why didn't He choose His mother or His disciples? Moved by this, she and her husband started a work to reach out to prostitutes and women working in "gentlemen's bars" around the city. The Magdalene Project, as it became known, has since spread all over the nation.

The person of peace is a person of reputation—sometimes good, sometimes bad—who has a wide circle of influence. The church is usually started in that person's home.

How might this work itself out in today's world? One example could be found in the workplace. Let's assume you have just started a new job, and after a couple of weeks, one of your coworkers says, "On Fridays after work, a group of us goes out for a drink to relax after the week. Would you like to join us?" This person is opening up his circle of influence to you, and at this point you have two choices. You could say, "Thanks, but I don't drink." Or you could accept the invitation, order a beer or a soft drink (no one will care which beverage you choose), and become a welcome part of the group.

The person of peace principle is clearly illustrated in the New Testament. These are people of reputation (good or bad) who are open to your message. Cornelius, a God-fearing Roman centurion well-known for his generosity to the Jewish people, invited Peter and his companions into his home (Acts 10). Similarly, in Lydia's story, although nothing tells us that she was seeking the God of Israel, she opened her home to Paul after hearing his message (Acts 16). The woman at the well had a bad reputation, yet her testimony opened the door of salvation to her entire village (John 4).

ENJOY THE HOSPITALITY THAT GOD PROVIDES

*Don't move around from home to home. Stay in one place,
eating and drinking what they provide. Don't hesitate to
accept hospitality, because those who work deserve their
pay. If you enter a town and it welcomes you, eat whatever
is set before you.*

—LUKE 10:7-8, NLT

This passage tells us not to move from home to home, but
rather to stay in the home of the person of peace, eating and
drinking what is set before us. Both verses emphasize the importance of eating.

We realized the significance of not moving from home to
home when the person of peace for one of our groups lived in
a low-income housing project. We were concerned about asking this person to host us in her home, so we chose to meet in
the home of one of her neighbors. The neighbor had been a
Christian for a few years, and she had a nice, orderly home with
Christian music playing softly in the background. But the meeting was a disaster. None of the person of peace's friends or family
came. As soon as we moved the gathering back to the person of
peace's home, many attended and many found the Lord.

This verse goes on to say, "Eat whatever is set before you."
This is significant because eating with people creates relationship. When you accept someone's hospitality, it implies that you
accept that person and his or her culture. Sometimes you may
not like the food that people provide, but it is important to eat
it anyway; if you turn it down it may be taken personally, not
just as a rejection of their food.

It's also important to note that up until now, you have not preached or proclaimed the Kingdom in any way. You have only become a friend. Jesus frequently shared meals with people in their homes. He even invited Himself to Zacchaeus's home!

TRUST GOD TO ANSWER YOUR PRAYERS

Heal the sick, and tell them, "The Kingdom of God is near you now."
—LUKE 10:9, NLT

When you enter a new community, you are looking for the opportunity to bring people face-to-face with a supernatural God. And there is nothing like answered prayer to accomplish that goal.

As you get to know the person of peace, you can ask what needs he or she is concerned about. Is anyone sick in this person's family? Are there financial challenges? Are there relationship problems? How is this person's work situation? Once you identify the needs, you put your faith on the line and pray. And then you watch God respond to outrageous faith.

It is interesting to note that Jesus and the apostles often found people of peace in a supernatural way—usually through a dramatic answer to prayer or demonstration of the power of the Spirit.

All over the world today, believers are moving in "prophetic evangelism," or "power evangelism." This means that they are deliberately asking the Lord to lead them to someone they can pray for or touch with the gospel. These believers feel led to pray for the very specific needs of those they encounter. They often use one of the spiritual gifts referred to in 1 Corinthians 12, such as a word of knowledge or prophecy. They see healings (physical or emotional) and other answers to prayer.

A friend of ours once heard the Lord speak to her about a woman she happened to be seated next to on a park bench. She turned to the woman and said, "You have just come out of a psychiatric unit, haven't you?" It turned out that the lady had indeed just recently been released from the hospital, where she had been treated for severe depression. She was feeling lost and wondering what to do with her life. Amazed by the accuracy of the word of knowledge our friend had shared, this woman began to talk about her fears and concerns, and our friend was able to lead her to Jesus.

Once the Kingdom of God has been demonstrated in this way, it is easy to ask the person of peace if she has friends or family members who might be interested in hearing about a God who is changing lives. Suddenly, you may find yourself cooperating with the Holy Spirit in the birth of another church.

When the Lord led us to start a church in one of the low-income housing projects about twenty minutes from our home, we gathered together a team to pray for the area for several months. We prayer walked around the area, claiming it for the Kingdom, although most of our praying was done on an individual basis.

One day we happened to be driving nearby, and on impulse decided to stop and prayer walk the neighborhood again. We were specifically asking the Lord that we would meet our person of peace. As we were walking and praying, a torrential downpour surprised us so we ran to take shelter under a balcony with two women who turned out to be sisters. We started talking with these women, and they inquired what we were doing in their neighborhood.

We explained that we were praying for the area and asked if we could come by occasionally to pray about the needs in their family. They immediately agreed, and so for the next few weeks, we dropped in to pray for them every few days, staying just fifteen minutes or so. It wasn't long before we were seeing very specific answers to prayer. When God shows up and answers prayer, it gives you the right to talk about the Kingdom of God!

We soon realized that one of the sisters, Rosa, was our person of peace. She has a heart as big as Texas, loving and welcoming everyone. Our next step was to have Rosa bring some of her friends and family members together for a weekly meeting at her home. She very quickly became a Christian, and many of her family members did the same. We met families in several other homes in the complex, too, and within a year, Rosa's apartment was crowded every week with thirty to forty people sitting on the stairs, on the floor, everywhere. Neighbors began telling us that the area was changing, that there was less violence and some of the drug dealers had moved out.

Another interesting side benefit was the effect it had on friends of our own children, non-Christian teenagers who went with us to help with the younger ones. These teens were profoundly touched and moved by what they saw, and for some of them, time spent at Rosa's became a large part of their own journey toward salvation.

When you step out in faith to follow the principles in Luke 10, you *will* begin to see what you long for—new disciples and churches planted in the harvest.

14

STORIES FROM THE HARVEST

THERE'S NOTHING LIKE a story to turn a principle from theory into practice. The road from the head to the heart is a long one. The journey from the heart to the head is much shorter! Following are some stories straight from the harvest. These are not sanitized success stories. They are real-life, raw and messy, sometimes gut-wrenching tales told by ordinary people.

If you read them closely, you will also find that most of them illustrate Luke 10 principles. These new churches are usually built on a foundation of prayer; often a person of peace is key to reaching a community; and an answer to prayer may open the door for an explanation of the good news of Jesus.

Is a small group of homeless people finding Jesus of any real significance? It is to them! How about a group of moms with young families? As these stories multiply, they inspire others to listen to God and respond to Him by going out into the harvest too.

Read them and enjoy!

THE CHURCH AT TABLE NUMBER TWO

Bill Hoffman writes:

"Would you like us to pray for you about something?" I asked. Immediately the eyes of our waitress opened wide as she blurted out her answer in the affirmative. It was Tuesday evening and our men's accountability group had gathered for our regular meeting at a local coffee shop. For the past several months we had been offering to pray for those who waited on us. Most of the requests we received were fairly superficial. "My grandma is sick." "I have a test coming up tomorrow." "My boyfriend needs a job." But when "Fran" began to share her issues with us, it was like someone had backed up a dump truck to our booth and emptied its contents out onto our table. Her daughter was suffering from cancer. A grandson had been born with serious medical problems. And her adult son had been thrown out of his home along with his three-year-old daughter. Fran had sacrificed financially to set them up in an apartment nearby, but they had no furniture and her son had no job. She was working two full-time jobs to support them all and was still sinking quickly into debt.

"We will certainly pray for all of these requests," I promised, "and we will see what else we can do to help." Over the next few days we managed to come up with some leads for employment for her son and found a few items of furniture for them to use. On the following Tuesday, Fran, who turned out to be a manager at the restaurant, was again our waitress, and once again we offered to pray for her. By the third week, Fran was sitting down with us in our booth and joining us in our prayers. This was the evening she dropped the bombshell that has revolutionized the way we've been doing church.

"Thank you so much for your prayers and for all your help," she gushed with a huge smile. "You guys have meant so much to me! I look forward to Tuesday night all week. Other people have invited me to their churches, but they all meet on Sunday mornings when I am always working. So God brought you guys to me on Tuesday nights." After spreading out her hands toward the rest of us sitting at the table, she joyfully declared, "This is my church!"

I'm afraid the first thought that crossed my mind was, *No it's not! This is a men's accountability group*. But the Lord quickly revealed to me that this was exactly what we had been praying for. For months we had been moved to fervently pray for "workers for the harvest," asking the Lord to specifically connect us to a "man of peace." These prayer directives came from our study of Luke 10:1-9. It dawned on us that we had just found a "man of peace," even though the "man" was definitely a female, and her house was not a house at all but rather a restaurant.

At first we attempted to invite her to our weekly house church fellowship that meets at my home on Sunday evenings. However, her schedule made this impossible and her own apartment was in a community some twenty miles away. So we just resigned ourselves to the fact that the Lord of the harvest had morphed our men's accountability group into a rather unique church.

Early on, Fran provided the name for this special gathering when she related to us a conversation she'd had with a fellow employee.

"You're doing drugs, aren't you?" Fran had asked one of her coworkers with a tone of compassion rather than accusation. "Don't try to deny it, because I've been around and I know the signs."

The young waitress just stared back at her through dilated, bloodshot eyes, waiting for the expected pronouncement of her termination.

"Don't worry," Fran continued, "I'm not going to fire you or turn you in to the police. I'm just concerned about you, and I know that whatever your problems are, this is not the answer. Jesus is the answer! We need to change your work schedule so you can be here on Tuesday nights. Then you can go to church with me."

Feeling somewhat relieved, the drug-addicted waitress responded by asking, "Where is your church located?"

As her face erupted into a huge smile, Fran pointed over to a booth in the corner of the restaurant and proudly proclaimed, "Table number two!"

From that point on, our gathering has been called the Church at Table Number Two.

Not long after Fran revealed to us that our gathering was in fact a church, she told us she had a surprise for us. She then excused herself from the table, went back into the kitchen, and brought out the cook and his assistant. After we all introduced ourselves, we asked the two men what we could do to help them.

"We have heard all that you have done to help Fran," began one of the Hispanic men, speaking in heavily accented English. "We both live in very small apartments and have very large families. Could you perhaps find us some furniture? We especially need beds for our children."

"I don't know if we can help you," I responded. "But I know who can. Jesus was the one who found help for Fran. Would it be okay if we asked Jesus to help you, too?"

Within a couple of weeks we had found some used furniture for these men, and we began to connect every Tuesday evening with the cook. He led us to another family in a nearby community who was also in dire need of help: a young, recently widowed Hispanic woman with three young children and very little means to support them. We soon began meeting regularly in this woman's home, taking the love of Jesus with us and doing what we could to help. Before long we were also traveling regularly to the cook's home and "doing church" with him and his family. The cook, his wife, and her mother have all placed their faith in Jesus, and God continues to open up doors through them into the Hispanic community. This has all been truly amazing to us since neither my wife nor I speak any Spanish, and most of these new acquaintances speak little if any English. I'm not even a fan of Mexican food, but God's Word tells us to "eat whatever is set before you" (Luke 10:8, NIV). So I'm learning to sacrifice my tongue and digestive tract for the greater good of reaching out to a people group in our area who are in desperate need of the gospel of love. We are learning that the love of Jesus can break through any ethnic barriers.

I believe it is significant to note that not one of these individuals has ever attended our own home gathering. However, we are perfectly content with this development. It's not that we wouldn't love to have them; it's just that they would most likely have a difficult time adjusting to our way of doing things, not to mention our food. Besides, the Lord has been teaching us to change the direction of our focus. For years our goal was to grow our home gathering to the point where it would be obvious we needed to split off and start another group. We would then commission a few of our members and send them out to plant the next church in another home. It's not that this concept is terribly wrong; it's just terribly slow. Meanwhile, the harvest is ripe and waiting.

These days we are not asking people to join the group that meets in our home. When we come across a person of peace, or discover someone interested in doing simple church, or lead someone to the Lord, our first instinct is to plant a new church in that person's home. We ask them to gather together their family and friends, especially those who are not yet Christians or who don't attend church anywhere else, and we proceed to help them plant a church in the surroundings they know best, where Jesus can make the biggest difference: in their homes and workplaces. The results have been truly remarkable. But why should we be surprised? This is exactly how Jesus taught us to do it.

STREET CHURCH

John Lunt writes:

A little over two years ago, I attended a simple church for the first time. I wasn't looking to change churches or anything. But it was so life giving, I never returned to the traditional church I had been attending.

Soon after that, a network of simple churches in our area conducted a workshop for people interested in starting a church. They talked more about making disciples than starting churches.

That's no big deal! I thought to myself. *I can do that.*

During that class, I sensed God directing me to go downtown every Saturday and start making disciples. The following Saturday I took a hundred pairs of socks downtown and started giving them out to the homeless.

That's when I met George. George was homeless, but he loved Jesus and we connected. Several other homeless people hung around him—he was our person of peace for that community. George used to have a job making over $100,000 per year, but after some financial mismanagement, he ended up on the streets.

One day the Lord tapped him on the shoulder and told him, "This is your last chance to follow Me." George responded. Now he demonstrates the love of Christ more than anyone I know. He'll take the gloves off his hands to give to someone who needs them.

Over the weeks we connected with more people. We ended up with a core group of seven or eight people, although many others came occasionally. The transition to a church came naturally. We just started gathering.

In January of 2007, George told us, "I don't fit in anywhere else. This is my place!" Soon other people started thinking of it as church. So we became a church that met on the street in front of city hall.

George's life was transformed through this, and last year he left to go back to his family.

Let me paint a picture of a typical time together on the streets. Our gatherings included sharing a meal together, hanging out, and enjoying fellowship. We worshiped and studied the Word of God. Initially we went through John's Gospel, and then we studied Acts. Our Bible study involved reading a chapter a week and engaging in some vigorous discussion. Surprisingly, the main theme the Lord continued to bring up was that of dying to self, taking up our crosses, and following Jesus. We would end by praying for each other. We shared the gospel with people on the streets and prayed for them. Often we would distribute winter hats, socks, clothing, or cold water—whatever they might need at that time of year.

We focused on individuals, building them up as disciples of Christ and giving them hope that they could get out of their situation.

John, another core member, came every Saturday. He was on the streets because of mental health issues and some bad decisions. One night while he was riding with me, he told me he had been baptized twice but never understood it before. He was baptized because his mom wanted him to do it, not because he had a relationship with Jesus. He finally understood the gospel and wanted to be baptized.

John was the first person we baptized. Ben, one of my friends, really began investing time in him and discipling him. A few months ago we did a study on being filled with the Holy Spirit, and John was profoundly changed through this. A pickle factory was willing to give homeless guys a job—a shot at a new life. We got John some clothes, and he moved in with Ben. He's working steadily, attending a simple church each week, and studying the Word of God. Jesus has changed his life.

Last January, the Lord impressed upon us that we needed to spend some time washing the feet of homeless people. They really got into it. Someone had given one of our homeless guys, Bill, twenty dollars. He felt such compassion during the foot washing that he gave his twenty dollars to someone else in need. Then he panicked because he had given all his money away! I could have gone to the ATM to replace it, but I heard the Lord telling me not to. He wanted to teach Bill to trust Him. I told Bill to walk up and down the block and pray until he felt peace. In just a few minutes, he was flooded with joy.

The following week, he commented, "Every time I turn around, people give me money. I've been given over a hundred dollars since we last met!"

Bill is now off the streets and helping a friend to remodel a house. He currently leads the group and has become quite a Bible scholar, spending a lot of time in the Word.

We Christians can learn to get out of the four walls of either the institutional church or the house church. I started with servant evangelism because it was what I knew. If I were doing it again, I wouldn't use servant evangelism. The guys we work with don't believe they can reproduce servant evangelism because they can't buy things to give away. In the future, I will trust God that He will do miraculous things when we pray for people. If we want to reproduce disciples, then we have to model evangelism in a way they can duplicate. Any disciple can learn to have faith that God will respond to their prayers.

The main group ended last month because most of the core members have jobs or are off the street. Two or three of them, led by Bill, continue to meet in front of city hall. God told me my time there was finished. I believe we did what He wanted us to accomplish. That's the great thing about simple church. When it has run its course, there's no reason to continue it artificially. It is easy to move on to God's next thing when you don't have a payroll or a mortgage.

MOM CHURCH

Jamie Richardson writes:

When my husband and I bought our first home in September of last year, we did so with the intent of starting our first house church. We are ecstatic about it and have anxiously awaited the new neighborhood's completion so we can really reach out. But being a full-time at-home mom with two toddlers, I needed something to occupy my time until then.

I found a Web site called meetup.com. I just typed in my zip code and my interest in meeting other moms for playgroups. I found one right here in my city, and I signed up. Since then I have moved from being a member to being an assistant organizer.

We are a group of thirty-five moms and growing. We have all become friends and get together several times a week. As is inevitable in the Bible Belt, eventually religion came up. Being relatively new to the organic church movement, I was convinced that I would be crucified for my "outside the box" thinking. But I laid it out there. I told these ladies about our transition from the traditional congregational church and our heart for an organic, home-based ministry. I got some head nods, but that was about it.

Then a whisper came to my right ear, and the lady sitting next to me started telling me her story about being raised Christian but not really knowing that she even believed in Jesus as the Messiah anymore. My first impulse was to "bring her back" to the truth. But I stopped myself. I shut up and I listened to her pour out her heart, soul, and struggles. That night I got a big thank-you e-mail from her.

The next day I got an e-mail from another mom who is Jewish and married to a Catholic. Within a week I had conversations with three other moms who all said they had been raised in church but had left for one reason or another. And it hit me. I was right smack-dab in the middle of organic church, and I was too busy focusing on my next-door neighbor to see the hearts of my new friends.

So I invited all of these ladies over for a discussion group. I assured them it would not be a Bible study, because a lot of them don't even believe in and follow the Bible. We would just discuss our hearts, beliefs, and struggles.

At our first meeting, those in attendance included a lady who was raised Catholic but has not attended church in years, a lady whose father was a Baptist preacher and who married an Assembly of God man, a lady who has never been to a church service but is a self-proclaimed "seeking soul," and my friend who was raised Christian but had no belief in the Messiah. Quite a group! And it went great.

We decided that each meeting would have a discussion topic. Our next one will be about how we define our role as wife and mother. We will each bring whatever it is that we use as our guidebook. (One lady is bringing *Nanny 911!*)

But then came that question, "Jamie, would you mind looking up some stuff in the Bible and just telling me where to look so I can come with some good thoughts? I mean, I have a Bible, but I don't know how to use it."

Umm. Sure, I can do that!

What I am learning is that "organic church" is just that. It is natural progression from relationship to faith community. It is not about converting everyone we see and meet; it is about making friends. God will do His work in His timing. It is my job to be available and willing when that door is open. I don't have to shove it open and throw my Bible in the crack so it can't close back. I do believe that God put us in this house to start a church within our neighborhood, but who am I to limit Him to "just" my neighbors? I understand now that truly organic churches can start anywhere and with anyone that God sets in our path.

Here is an e-mail update on Jamie's situation:

I thought you might be blessed by some of the new things going on in our lives and ministry. "House church" is not at all what we thought it would be when we first set out on this adventure.

First, as far as our actual house church, we still "only" have one other couple meeting with us. We have had several others asking questions, but no one else has made the plunge. We have found ourselves being mentors for the other couple, though. God has really used us. They have suffered a number of trage-dies that we have previously been through, and it has been really wonderful to have a front-row seat for watching their marriage and family grow.

Second, I continue to make and deliver monthly baskets to new neighbors in our fast-growing neighborhood. We invite everyone to a big meal every other month. We had about twenty people join us on Saturday. It is wonderful to connect people to one another and to get their stories. Most people are so untrust-ing these days that it is really cool when people realize we really aren't trying to sell anything or get anything out of them; we are just being good neighbors. We always have people ask if they can come to the next "eating." We are going to have to split into multiple groups in multiple houses because our gatherings are growing so quickly.

Third is our spiritual discussion group. I finally received my first complaint, but it is about as good a complaint as I could receive: "Jamie, can we do them more often?" My house had gotten pretty full. A couple of meetings ago we had thirty-seven moms and kids here! So we are now going to start three meetings—one in the morning for those who nap in the afternoon, one in the afternoon for those with kids in school, and one in the evening for working moms. *Incredible!* We'll have a "topic of the month" to discuss, and then each set of people will also exchange ideas on an Internet message board. I cannot believe how much this is catching on. These moms have a real desire to share their thoughts and spiritual journeys with other moms, but they've never been given the opportunity without feeling judged or "converted." To have women raised Catholic, Baptist, Methodist, Anglican, nondenominational, atheist, and agnostic all get together in my living room to say, "I just don't know what I believe about . . ." is an amazing ministry opportunity! I just sit there and spur on the conversation with questions.

Finally—and this was *huge* for me—last night, three of us got together for coffee. An agnostic, a former Catholic, and I were all sitting there talking about how amazed we all are by these spiritual discussion groups.

One of them looked at me and said, "You know, I think I know what you believe, but I don't think you've ever tried to sell

your opinion. Where are you on your own spiritual journey?"
I had prayed for this. I have wanted this, but I also wanted it
to happen very naturally. I told them that for the first time in
my life that I can remember, I am very, very happy with where
I am on my spiritual journey. I am content and growing. I have
released myself from man-made rules about where I am supposed to be and what I am supposed to be, and I have found
where God wants me to be.

I said, "To put it plainly, I believe that Jesus Christ is the
Messiah. And I have a personal, daily relationship with Him to
prove it." Then I dropped it.

They both looked at me with this shocked look on their
faces, and then the agnostic said, "Then why haven't you tried
to convert me?" I said, "That is not my job. Your spiritual journey is between you and God. My job is to walk my journey and
allow you to see it."

I think that blew their minds.

Anyway, that is where we are: blessed, to say the least. As I
said, this house church thing is not what we thought it would
be, but there is more "real ministry" going on right now than
we've ever had!

CUBAN CHURCH

Willie Butler writes:
Fall 2007

Juan is seventy-one years old. He is a political refugee from
Cuba, where he spent thirty years in prison before coming to
the United States. I first met him when I worked for a refugee
resettlement agency. I built a good relationship with him and
he knew about my faith in Christ.

The leadership team of our network of simple churches had been praying for the Cuban community for more than a year. Cubans are passionate about baseball and often asked for a game with Americans. With the help of members from the various simple churches in our network, we assembled a team to play a series of games with the Cubans. I gave a flyer to Juan, and he passed it out to the community living in his apartment complex.

The baseball series was great fun, and yes, we lost every game. More importantly, we were able to have an intentional ministry. At the first game I was able to explain that we wanted them to know Christ, and that He wanted to give them more than political and social freedom.

The games allowed time for proclamation and prayer, one-on-one relationships, and the opportunity to make house visits. Two friends and I visited Juan and his roommate at their home. We explained the gospel and they both listened to the Good News intently. Juan's roommate felt he wanted to continue counting the cost of following Jesus. Juan, however, was more than ready to submit his life to Christ. After confessing his sin and need for Jesus, he asked Christ to save him. I remember him praying, "Jesus, my whole life was an error."

I've been amazed at the work of the Holy Spirit in Juan's life. Juan's faith is tremendous, and it challenges and encourages me. I wish you could see how his life has been transformed. One major fruit of the Spirit is the peace that Juan has in his circumstances. He hasn't seen his wife in three years; he just underwent bypass surgery on his heart, and he has numerous health problems. The others in his community ask why he is so content and hopeful. He testifies, "The Lord is with me."

Juan was our person of peace for that community; he opened his apartment for an evangelistic Bible study. We focus on discipleship, using the Gospels to emphasize knowing Jesus above all else. We teach the new believers to hear God and obey Him. At Easter, Juan was baptized. The water was cold, but nothing was stopping this old man.

Christ put something in my heart for these Cubans over the past couple of years. Through all the loving, sharing, praying, God was working to draw Juan to Himself. Now my friend has become my brother.

Update, summer 2008:

We have played a couple of baseball games with the Cubans this summer too. They are great times. The first game we held them scoreless for the last five innings. Somehow they still won 20–3. But about twenty Cubans and twenty-five Americans ate pizza together and had some great fellowship after the game. A single mom, a couple, and a single man expressed interest in the Bible studies we have at the Cuban apartment complex.

The simple church/evangelistic Bible study in that community is growing. The Lord's work is astounding. Last week we met in Uvaldo's home and five Cubans were there. Juan and a couple of others naturally lead out in song, testimony, and prayer. It is exciting for the believers to have people from their own community gathered.

BLANKITY BLANK CHURCH

Ross Rohde writes:

Sunday, June 24, 2007

My wife, Margi, and I were staying in the guest cottage of

some longtime friends. My friend asked me if I would like to attend a new Bible study he was hosting. He mentioned there would be some non-Christians there. As we talked, I told him how I do inductive Bible study with non-Christians and new believers: I keep it simple by drawing four symbols representing four questions:

- A Bible: What does it say?
- A question mark: What does it mean?
- A lightbulb: What are you going to do about it?
- A mouth: Who are you going to tell?

My friends were a bit dubious that this would work—it was too simple.

Two couples, one of them Korean American, and two single women showed up at our host's home for the Bible study. The Korean American man, a powerfully built and tall man I'll call Mr. X, was very aggressive in personality and openly abusive to his wife, who cowered in his presence. He also spoke with a tremendous amount of profanity. I was surprised at his blatant hostility. I was also surprised that he was so openly angry and profane at a Bible study. Usually people try to put on a good face on such occasions. At least he was honest.

We ate some snacks out on the deck, and then our hosts invited us to come into the living room. They introduced everyone and then presented me as the one leading the Bible study. This was a surprise! I had only mentioned my ideas as something they might try sometime. However, since my method is simple and doesn't require preparation, I explained the four symbols and their questions, and had the participants find the first chapter of John's Gospel.

There was plenty of participation and discussion. We were probably twenty minutes into the study, when suddenly Mr. X spoke in a gruff and hostile voice.

"*Blankity blank*, I want to know Jesus."

I was taken aback. "What did you say?" I asked.

He again said, "*Blankity bleep blank blank*, I want to know Jesus."

So I began to explain the gospel as simply and clearly as possible. He seemed confused by even this simple presentation. I could tell he was an intelligent man, but he just couldn't seem to get the gospel. I was beginning to wonder if demons were trying to prevent him from understanding.

Finally our host said, "Mr. X, I had some of the same problems you do when I first heard about Jesus. But I learned that it was really just about surrender. I needed to surrender to Jesus."

Mr. X responded, "*Blank it*, I can *blankity bleep* understand that. I want to *bleep bleep bleep* surrender to Jesus."

I stood up and walked over to Mr. X and commanded him to stand up. This was not my usual behavior, but for some reason I just did it. He stood up. I looked him in the eye.

I asked him forcefully, "Do you want Jesus?"

He said, "*Bleepity bleep*, I do!"

I asked again, "Do you really want Jesus?"

"*Blankity bleep blank blank*, I do!"

I said, "Welcome to the Kingdom."

This tough guy then began to cry. The next thing I said was, "Mr. X, I want to start a church at your house. When are we going to do that?"

He said, "Tomorrow at 5:00." He then gave me his card with his address on it. I suggested he invite his friends.

We did meet at his house the next day at 5 p.m., and on many Mondays after that. He and his wife invited many of their friends, particularly those in the Korean American community. Some of these people were Christians and some were not. A few came to Christ.

In the process, it became abundantly clear to my church planting partners and me that Mr. X did indeed have a significant demonic problem. We began praying with him and casting out some of the demons. This was a long and painful process. His wife, Mrs. X, was also set free from some demonic problems. Mrs. X in particular began to grow rapidly in her faith. I developed a personal discipleship relationship with Mr. X. However, this relationship was somewhat sporadic, due to Mr. X's personality.

As the demonic problems were dealt with, Mr. X's personality changed dramatically. He was considerably more peaceful and friendly. He swore less. He began to treat his wife with kindness and respect. He also mentioned that he could feel an internal change and now felt more peaceful and lighter. However, before we had finished dealing with all the demonic issues in his life, he became content with the change as it was and resistant to further ministry. We warned him this was not wise, but it was his decision.

In the meantime, one of the families that Mr. and Mrs. X had introduced us to invited us to meet in their home. The wife was already a Christian but her husband, who was a European businessman working in the United States, was not. Within a few months, this man had a significant conversion. I used this opportunity to train three other church planters.

This church initially did well, but the wife kept referring to religious practices that she was accustomed to in her former church. We told her we preferred to keep things as simple and easy as possible, but if she could find these practices in the Bible we would do them. Of course, they were not actually biblical practices but "religious" ones.

Over time, however, the wife began to take her husband to her church because she felt they had a "real" pastor who was trained in a seminary. I didn't tell her that I had much more official training and education than her pastor because I didn't want to support the idea that somehow education makes us better. What really counts is the depth of relationship with Jesus. Finally this woman cut off our relationship, though we ended on a cordial note. I know she felt our group was not "religious" enough.

In the meantime, Mr. X began to manifest demonic problems more and more strongly. We were in contact with his wife, but he was becoming increasingly evasive. We tried to warn him he was on a dangerous path. He just became harder to pin down. Mrs. X reported that he was getting very aggressive and abusive again. In a meeting with both of them, we suggested they separate temporarily while we worked with Mr. X to get him all the help he needed. Instead of this, he decided to take his wife and move to Korea. We have talked by phone with Mrs. X since then, but not with Mr. X.

Lessons learned:

1. Religious Christians can be very disruptive to simple churches that have started among non-Christians. We

need to be very careful they don't bring their religion with them. Personally I prefer to work with non-Christians and new Christians in church planting.

2. We needed to learn more about spiritual warfare. It would be ideal to have trained resource people among our network of church planters who could help in these situations. However, we can only clean out demons that the person wants cleaned out.

PICANTE CHURCH

Ross Rohde writes again:

Church starting January 20, 2008, San Rafael, CA

San Rafael is an affluent community on the Marin Peninsula on the other side of the Golden Gate Bridge from San Francisco. The Canal District contains over 20 percent of San Rafael's population in a few densely packed blocks of apartment buildings. This is where the poor of San Rafael live, separated by an invisible but very real social barrier. Marin needs the cheap labor of these people in order to function. However, most of the affluent people of Marin don't want to have to live with them, and they want to see them as little as possible. Marin County residents tend to speak of the Canal District with disdain and sometimes even fear.

A few years ago, God gave Marian Engelland a vision for a multiplying network of indigenous churches in the Canal District. She and her husband, Ryan, moved there to minister to the Hispanic immigrant community. They live in an expensive yet tiny apartment next door to the people they came to work with.

Over time, Ryan and Marian led one of their neighbors to the Lord. This man introduced them to his brother, who also came to the Lord. This brother, in turn, introduced Ryan to Jose. Jose came to the Lord when his wife had an affair and left him brokenhearted.

In January, Ryan and I began to meet Jose every Sunday morning for breakfast at the Picante Restaurant in the Canal. This was difficult for Jose because he worked long hours, often more than twelve hours per day and sometimes seven days a week.

Jose began to grow in his faith. He shared his faith at work and became known for his Christian walk. He invited others to Picante, though they never showed up. He even asked some of the people he knew at the Picante to join us.

In the meantime we began to mention Picante Church at the English-as-a-second-language class Marian had started at the local community center. My friends and I shared the gospel after class with anyone who was interested. However, no one from the class ever came to Picante. That is, until we started prayer walking. On July 12, a couple of Canal Ministry teammates and I walked around the outside of the Canal District and prayed. The next day Ryan and I did the same thing.

On July 20 two men from the language class showed up at Picante. We invited them to breakfast and asked them to share their spiritual journey. Jaime shared that he had grown up in an evangelical family in Guatemala but had never become a Christian. He was afraid that he would never be good enough. Jose and I shared that Jesus would accept him just as he was. He responded that if he became a Christian, he would fail and disappoint God. We told him that Jesus could deal with that, too. We shared the gospel clearly and we challenged him to accept Jesus. He was very interested but still chose to wait.

Eduardo was a quiet man. He shared that he struggled with anger, bitterness, and a desire for revenge due to the fact that two men had murdered his father. He knew these emotions were harming him and he wanted to be free. We invited Jaime and Eduardo to come back the next week.

The next week Jose had to work. Ryan and I were hoping that Jaime and Eduardo would return, but they didn't. Instead, one of the other students, Alejandro, a dedicated Christian from the language class, showed up. We invited him to sit with us.

After a bit he said, "I came to tell you about Eduardo. He came to Christ!"

We were elated and asked him to tell us more.

"He was in the army in Guatemala, you know. He was an assassin and knew how to make bombs."

I used to live in Guatemala and knew of the Guatemalan Army's reputation, especially a special forces unit called the Kaibiles.

"Was Eduardo a Kaibil?" I asked Alejandro.

"Yes, he was." A cold chill ran down my back. Kaibiles were nasty characters and very capable and efficient killers.

"Continue with the story."

"Well, Eduardo came to Jesus, and his anger and hatred just left him. Jesus filled him with peace."

I told Ryan the news, since Picante Church is conducted in Spanish, and Ryan can't usually keep up with the excited, rapid-fire Spanish.

Ryan was excited for Eduardo. He said, "Now we just need to see Jaime come to Jesus."

"He already has," said Alejandro. "Eduardo called Jaime right away. He told him, 'Jaime, you are always waiting to get good enough. You are afraid to enter the race for fear you are going to lose. How will you know what will happen if you never try? This is wonderful. Just do it.' So Jaime became a Christian too.

"You know Roberto and Juanita from class?" Alejandro continued. "Roberto became a Christian a week ago when you guys preached the gospel."

"Wow, now we need to see Juanita become a Christian," Ryan commented.

"Oh, she already is. Not only that, but they are also sharing the gospel with one of Roberto's cousins."

Since then, we have been discipling Jaime, Eduardo, and Alejandro, along with Jose, at Picante Church. They come as often as they can. However, the instability and poverty of a day laborer's life requires that they take a job any time it is offered. Jaime brought one of his cousins to Picante. He also brought a friend to class so that he would hear the gospel. In the meantime, we are teaching them how to read the Bible, pray, and minister to one another as acts of direct obedience to Jesus. We also shared with them 2 Timothy 2:2 and suggested that they should begin to tell other people everything they hear from us. This would be living what they learned in 2 Timothy 2:2.

15

TELLING STORIES

JESUS HIMSELF WAS a master storyteller. He frequently communicated using stories and everyday ideas His listeners were familiar with to convey truths in a way that those with ears to hear could understand. He spoke about crops and sheep farming; He gave stories of masters and servants; He used household analogies—yeast, salt, lost coins.

Wherever you go in the world, people love to hear stories. Every culture has its own repertoire of stories that somehow serves to distinguish and endorse its identity. Families have stories that are passed down from generation to generation. Stories help to ground and give meaning to our lives.

Stories are also powerful communicators of ideas. Ivan Illich, an Austrian philosopher and anarchist, was once asked how to change society. His reply was something to this effect: "Neither revolution nor reformation can ultimately change a society. Rather, you must tell a new powerful tale, one so persuasive that it sweeps away the old myths and becomes the preferred story. If you want to change a society, then you have to tell an alternative story."

People love to tell their own stories. A friend of ours, Tim Pynes, tried an experiment. One day he sat at a coffee shop with a sign that stated, "I'll buy you a cup of coffee if you let me tell you my story about God." Over a period of several hours, only one person responded. The next day he moved to another coffee shop with a different sign. This one said, "I'll buy you a cup of coffee if you tell me your story about God." People lined up to tell him their stories. Many were in tears and thanked him profusely for listening.

Whenever we get together with a new group of people, we usually begin by asking everyone to tell the story of their spiritual journey. One of the first times we did this was with a dozen or so people in their late teens and early twenties.

The first girl to share told the group that she had been sent to Texas to live with her father after an argument with her mother. Because she moved in the middle of a school year, some of her credits didn't transfer, and she found the additional schoolwork very difficult. Back in California with her mother, she had led the cheerleading team and was popular with many friends. She knew no one in Texas and became more and more depressed. One day she locked herself in the bathroom and lined up all of the pill bottles from the medicine cabinet in front of her. She had decided to take her own life. But before she did, she cried out to God, begging Him to reveal Himself to her if He existed—and God met her right then and there. A few days later, this girl met our daughter, Becky, and a few weeks later, she was telling her story in our meeting. Her story affected everyone there. There wasn't a dry eye in the place— cool teenage guys and all! It's easy to share about Jesus in a context like that.

Often your own story can also be a powerful tool in reaching out with the Good News. In *Church Planting Movements*, David Garrison writes about "John" in China, who taught a group of thirty farmworkers how to tell their stories and then encouraged them to share the stories with five people they were praying for. After the first week, only seventeen of the thirty had shared their stories, but one farmer had shared with eleven people. So at the next class, they each encouraged one another by sharing their experiences, and practiced telling their stories again. After two months, they had already started twenty groups that were becoming churches. After seven months, that number grew to over three hundred small groups and four thousand newly baptized believers. Just over a year after the experiment began, nine hundred house churches were meeting, with more than twelve thousand new Christians![1]

You can tell your spiritual story in a way that is understandable to a person who does not yet know Jesus, without implying that you have all of the answers. You also need to learn to tell your story in just two or three minutes for situations where that is more appropriate. Your personal story should answer the following three questions:

1. What was life like before you became a Christian (or before your faith became real to you)?

2. How did you meet Jesus?

3. How has Jesus changed your life?

Learning to share your story is a skill you will use time and time again in your conversations with unbelievers. Any story, or indeed any conversation, with not-yet-believers should never be couched in "Christianese." Words such as *salvation*, *redemption*—even *sin*—can be rephrased in such a way that someone with no Christian background is not left wondering what you are talking about. As you practice telling your story to others, you will find that not only does it become easy to tell, but also you can tell it in ways that always sound fresh.

You may even develop several different parts to your story that fit the different circumstances of the people around you. For example, if you are talking with someone who is dealing with a financial need, you might share about a time when God provided for you.

Over the years, we have developed a pattern for reaching out to unbelievers that seems to work well in a Western context and that involves the use of stories.

When people become followers of Jesus or show an interest in spirituality, we don't invite them to come to our church. Instead, we ask them to bring together a few of their friends so we can "explore spirituality" further. (You'll want to ask the Lord to help you find what buzzword works in any particular situation.) We prefer to meet in their homes and within their circles of influence and culture.

During our first meeting with the new group, we usually share a meal and then ask someone to tell us the story of his or her spiritual journey—a wonderfully nonthreatening way to get the conversation started. We try to give people plenty of time, asking questions to make sure we really understand what they are sharing. We've found that unbelievers are usually quite willing to open up their lives in this way. As we go around the room, everyone has an opportunity to share his or her story.

Storytelling is effective, because at the end of our first meeting, we have a very good idea of where each person stands spiritually. We know whether the people in the group have any church background and what their belief systems look like. We also ask people to pray for the needs of those in the group; we've found that if people pray right from the start—even before they become Christians—praying out loud is never a problem later. At the start of a new group, we may not know who these people are praying to, but we do know that *our* God takes pleasure in answering their prayers!

If it is a large group, it may take a couple of weeks for everyone to tell his or her story. Once everyone has shared, we talk about getting together again to further "explore spirituality." We let them know that we will provide a book for discussion, and the next week we bring an adequate number of an easy-to-read version of the Bible or New Testament.

For subsequent gatherings, we use a pattern based on Acts 2:42, in which the disciples "devoted themselves to the apostles' teaching and to the fellowship, to the breaking of bread and to prayer" (NIV).

1. We start with a meal—either potluck dishes or carryout food, depending on what is most suitable for the group. With teens or students, pizza might be more appropriate.

2. We share the "God events" of the past week. Even those who don't know the Lord will talk about ways He has worked in their lives. Theologically this is a concept known as "prevenience"—God at work in our lives even before we hand them over to Him.

3. We spend some time in the Word using the question mark, lightbulb, and arrow method. The Gospel of John is a good place to start. The first chapter is not easy for everyone to understand, but we don't give people the answers. We let them dig out the meaning for themselves. The Word of God is living and active, and over the weeks, we watch it change people's lives.

4. We pray for each other. The importance of God answering prayers is one of the key principles in the Luke 10 passage. Those answered prayers open the door and allow us to talk about the Kingdom. It doesn't matter that they do not yet know Jesus. God delights in answering their prayers, and when He does, they do not stay unbelievers for long! It also provides the basis for "God events" to share the next week. For example, if someone shared in a previous week that he had difficulties with his boss, usually he will report back that the tensions have eased or he was able to have a good conversation about the things troubling him.

We once followed this approach with a group of people involved in various New Age practices. The first week, following a wonderful meal in the home of the person of peace, each of us shared the story of our spiritual journey. All of them were searching for God or some kind of meaning to life. The next week those who were interested went on to study the Gospel of John. It only took a few weeks before the group accepted the Bible as having authority. After six weeks of sharing together and talking about the first few verses of John chapter 1, we finally arrived at John 1:12: "As many as received Him, to them He gave the right to become children of God."

When we read this, someone in the group asked, "What does it mean to receive Him?" Another person offered her opinion: "I think to receive means to commit!" Some general discussion about this idea followed, and everyone agreed this was probably a good definition. Then we suggested that people take some time alone to talk with the Lord and tell Him they wanted to commit their lives to Him. People went to various parts of the house individually. When they came back together, many in the group had obviously met with God. There were tears and hugs. It was a very precious time!

The discipling process had begun even before these people became believers. The result was a church built out of the harvest.

16

MAKING DISCIPLES

WITHIN THIS MICROCHURCH MOVEMENT, we are learning that it is Jesus' job to build the church. Our call is to make disciples (Matthew 16:18; 28:19).

Discipleship describes the process of growth in our life with God. It often begins prior to making a commitment to the Lord. Before our daughter, Becky, left to serve with Youth With A Mission, she wanted to share the Lord with her non-Christian friends. She chose to have a going-away party and get rebaptized, inviting about fifty of her "closest friends" to our home. After we enjoyed a huge barbecue, Becky told her story, and we baptized her in our hot tub. She left for YWAM the next day, but we continued to work with some of her friends, most of whom were in their late teens and early twenties. We met with these kids regularly, shared our stories, discussed the Word, and prayed for one another. Then, after we finished our more overtly spiritual time together, we often played games like Pictionary late into the night.

Gradually, the kids began to change. We didn't tell them they needed to change—the Word of God is "living and active" (Hebrews 4:12, NASB), and it transforms people's lives. Their language cleaned up, some of them stopped smoking, and many told us they were no longer doing drugs or getting drunk. One by one, they asked to be baptized. At that point, we made sure they really understood what it means to give their lives to God, and if necessary, we helped them to do so.

Increasingly we have come to understand that becoming a disciple of Jesus has little to do with responding to an altar call or praying the sinner's prayer. It used to be that people believed in something before they belonged. But today, things are changing. People want to belong, and once they do, the believing gradually grows on them. The discipleship process begins even before they have given their lives to God. We love to watch people's lives change as they come to a greater understanding of what it means to move from the kingdom of darkness to the Kingdom of light.

Jesus never commanded us to plant churches. In fact, He didn't tell us to get converts, either! He told us to make disciples, and then *He* would build His church.

Second Timothy 2:2 encourages us to "teach these truths to other trustworthy people who will be able to pass them on to others" (NLT). Hebrews 5:12 says that those who have been Christians for a while ought to be teaching others.

As we saw in the great commission, Jesus told us to teach

the new disciple to obey all that He had commanded. Discipleship is not a body of knowledge to be learned. When we turn discipleship into a series of doctrines or teachings and holiness into a set of rules, we are robbing the new believer of relevant, authentic experience with God.

When we disciple new believers, we help them to live as followers of Jesus, transformed into His likeness. We teach them how to live holy lives of obedience to Him. As their friends, we answer their questions on real life issues and deal with concerns that are relevant to them, helping to make their faith vital and significant to their lives.

But before we seek to become holy, we must truly believe that it is what God has called us to pursue. Our holiness is through the forgiveness we received through Christ and the guidance we receive from God's Spirit living within us. Paul regularly exhorted the Christ followers of his day to live holy lives. Yet these days, despite our knowledge of this command, Americans dismiss a life of holiness. A Barna Group survey revealed that only one-third of adults (35 percent) believe that God expects them to become holy. We have to embrace the concept before we are likely to pursue it—for our own benefit, as well as for the benefit of those whom we wish to reach with the fullness of God's grace.[1]

The way you live your life with new believers is important (1 Corinthians 11:1), and the best way to disciple others is to answer their questions by giving them life lessons in knowing Him. How do people learn about prayer? They pray with you. How do people learn to love the principles in God's Word? They see that you love the Word and use its principles to guide your life. How do people learn how to lay down their lives for each other? They watch you doing it for them.

In turn, the new disciple then passes the discipleship on to others, and disciples multiply.

Again, we have to be careful what people see in our lives. For the past five years The Barna Group has tracked the percentage of adults who say that their faith—understanding it, committing to it, and living it every day—is their top priority in life. Sadly, only one out of every six born-again Christians (17 percent) claim that their faith in God is their highest priority.[2] We pass on the things that matter most to us. How much does your faith in Jesus matter to you?

Jesus taught His disciples not only in teaching sessions (which appeared to be very interactive, with discussion and questions and answers), but also by allowing them to participate in the rough-and-tumble of everyday life with Him. Jesus' disciples experienced the practical, daily outworking of His teaching. In Luke 10, we read that He gave the disciples instructions and sent them out to obey what He told them. Then He asked them to report back on what happened, and when they did, He gave them further teaching based on their experiences (verses 17-24).

People need to be trained and equipped in practical ways for life in the Kingdom. The idea of an apprenticeship is very appropriate here. Head knowledge is of little value; everything needs to be applicable to life. For example, if we are trying to teach a group about the spiritual gift of prophecy (Acts 2:17-18; 1 Corinthians 12:10), we ask them to get into pairs (preferably with someone they do not know) and to pray quietly for the other person. After a few minutes, they are to share any thoughts, pictures, or verses that have come to mind as they are praying. It always amazes us when we do this activity that usually 75 to 80 percent of the people have heard something from God that is very specific and applicable to the other person's situation. The more quickly a person moves into ministry, the faster that person will grow.

It is also important that the new believer learns to pass on what he or she is learning to others. In parts of China, discipleship chains are used to accomplish this. Curtis Sergeant, who worked among the house churches in China for many years, gives us this description:

> *A discipleship chain relationship is one that takes place outside of the regular church meeting. It is usually a one-on-two discipleship process. . . . The pattern is that a more mature believer disciples two others from within the congregation, each of whom disciples two others, who then disciple two others. Each discipling relationship involves mutual accountability for putting into practice scriptural truth that is learned and teaching what one has learned. This twofold accountability is extremely important. [This is taken very seriously. If the person being discipled has not put whatever the subject of the previous session was into practice and taught it to at least two others, they will cover the subject again until that has happened.]*
>
> *In order for this process to work, a person need be only one step ahead of the person whom he or she is discipling. . . .*
>
> *As a rule a discipleship chain . . . will not exceed four generations (plus the unbelievers that the last generation is "teaching").* [3]

Many churches are finding the pattern of Life Transformation Groups helpful. These groups, started by Neil Cole and described in his book *Cultivating a Life for God*, are made up of two to three people who commit to three things:

- reading significant portions of Scripture and comparing notes on them each week
- praying for friends who have not yet become Christians
- committing to a time of frank honesty based on answering personal accountability questions to one another each week

When a fourth person becomes a committed part of the group, it is split into two groups of two, and the movement spreads spontaneously.[4]

Recent research by Kent Smith of Abilene Christian University has shown that churches (whether simple or legacy) that use a very small group infrastructure like Life Transformation Groups in addition to larger times together are stronger and multiply faster than those that rely exclusively on the typical house church structure of ten to twenty people.[5]

The process of discipleship continues after the church is able to stand on its own. Mentoring, especially of the leaders, is important until the churches are well established and are multiplying.

One of the tragedies of many large-scale evangelistic efforts is that there is very little fruit to be found in the local churches a year later. There are no (or very few) new disciples. What has happened? People have made decisions, they have prayed a sinner's prayer, but they have not become disciples. In Luke

11:23, Jesus says, "He who does not gather with Me scatters." He also talked about new wine being put into new wineskins (Luke 5:37-38).

Although we can't name the nation for fear of exposing the people there to persecution, we have recently been involved in a situation where major evangelistic efforts have been followed up with simple churches. Those working in the follow-up process are trained to look for a person of peace and gather people around this person. On subsequent trips to these areas it has become clear that not only is the harvest being conserved, in subsequent months, it multiplies. Literally thousands of new churches are starting and spontaneously multiplying.

The large numbers responding in these large-scale evangelistic efforts are becoming disciples because they are being gathered into simple churches.

17

LEADERSHIP

It was a remarkable three-day meeting. About forty people, nearly all strong leaders from across the nation, were gathered together in our home for the sole purpose of waiting on God and listening to what He wanted to say to us. The room was arranged in two concentric circles. Most of the type A personalities—those who generally had strong, vocal opinions—sat on the inside circle. The quieter ones sat on the back row. On the last afternoon, as we waited on God, we sensed Him telling us to have everyone switch places so that those on the inner circle were now on the outside and vice versa. We then handed the floor over to those quieter ones, now the inner circle. Amazing wisdom flowed as they shared. It was as if the Lord said to us, "You have turned the room upside down.

If you will turn leadership upside down the way that you have turned this room upside down, Christians will again turn the world upside down" (Acts 17:6).

This was a compelling lesson about leadership. During our time together earlier that week, Bob Jones, a well-known prophet, phoned to tell us about a vision he had received for us. In the vision, he was in heaven and saw an incubator containing many eggs. His reaction was, "Great! More eagles for the Kingdom!" However, when the eggs hatched, the birds were not eagles but doves.

This vision had provoked much thought and insight from the group. Eagles represent tough, powerful leaders working alone. Doves fly in flocks, and as they fly, they all change direction simultaneously as if propelled by some external influence. Eagles are meat eaters; doves eat seeds and spread them by dropping them on the ground. Eagles characterize strength; doves represent gentleness and peace. Doves are a symbol of the Holy Spirit.

Nothing short of a radical transformation of leadership will suffice for the reformation that is unfolding before our eyes in this generation.

God is looking for leaders who walk with a limp: those who, like Jacob, have fought with God and surrendered to Him unconditionally (Genesis 32:24-32). God wants leaders who have learned from the disappointments and challenges of following Him through good times and bad. For leaders in the New Testament, their only promise was persecution, not professional perks and public praise. Their training came from the desert school of hard knocks, not the seminary of intellectual questioning. They valued the simplicity of Christ and expected to experience the power of the Holy Spirit in their work.

God is looking for those who are dead to their own ambitions. They have crucified any desire for the limelight, nailing to the cross their own agendas and ministries. They have no need to control. They are willing to go unrecognized, to be of no consequence in the world. They are looking for ways to lay down their lives for others.[1]

We love Wolfgang Simson's description of apostles as "weeping fathers, longing for their sons to overtake them."[2] There is no room for personal ambition because God does not share His glory. Our humility is the only way His glory will be seen by others. When we learn to boast in our weakness, the power of God is revealed (2 Corinthians 12:9).

In Matthew 20:25-27 (NLT), Jesus talks about leadership at some length. He says,

> You know that the rulers in this world lord it over their people, and officials flaunt their authority over those under them. But among you it will be different. Whoever wants to be a leader among you must be your servant, and whoever wants to be first among you must become your slave.

We do know what leadership looks like in the world; it is hierarchical and controlling. But Jesus says Kingdom leadership is the willing embrace of slavery and service. Jesus was the supreme example of this kind of servant leadership. He washed His disciples' feet and He served them. He laid down His life for others. He may even be the one who ultimately serves us at the marriage feast in heaven (Luke 12:37).

Paul gives us further insight into the nature of leadership when he says,

> *We were like children among you. Or we were like a mother feeding and caring for her own children. We loved you so much that we shared with you not only God's Good News but our own lives, too.*
> — I THESSALONIANS 2:7-8, NLT

New Testament leaders lead by example and are gentle and loving, ready to lay down their lives for those in their care (1 Peter 5:2-3).

Note the warning Jesus gives religious leaders of His day:

> *Don't let anyone call you "Rabbi," for you have only one teacher, and all of you are equal as brothers and sisters. And don't address anyone here on earth as "Father," for only God in heaven is your spiritual Father.*
> — MATTHEW 23:7-9, NLT

Yet in Christian circles today, we use titles like *pastor*, and we often place our leaders on a pedestal. When taken to an extreme, it becomes idolatry. This is not entirely the senior pastor's fault. The traditional church culture is set up in such a way that we are naturally inclined to view leaders in this way. Pastors are expected to act as CEOs rather than the servants they are called to be. As the paid professionals, pastors are not only expected to hear from God about the direction of the church, they are also expected to organize the programs, visit the sick, and have a perfect family life too! It is not surprising that in trying to live up to these impossible expectations, many end up shipwrecked morally, emotionally, or physically.

A few years ago, The Barna Group asked a national sample of churchgoing adults what duties they expected their pastors to perform with excellence. The list was jaw dropping: fifteen major, diverse responsibilities ranging from management to relationship building to teaching and scholarship. Companion studies indicated that there was no other person in a leadership position—in business, government, education, or nonprofit work—expected to master so many and such diverse obligations. Of course, such a job description is a recipe for failure. And it is important to realize that the job description has been concocted by churchgoers—it is not a list of expectations handed down by God through His words to us.

LEADERSHIP QUALIFICATIONS

What qualifications are leaders supposed to have? The Bible does not say they must have seminary training or a degree in theology. The focus is more on issues of character and lifestyle than anything else (1 Timothy 3:1-13; Titus 1:6-9). (This is not to say that academic qualifications are irrelevant—after all, Paul was highly educated according to the standards of his day. But we suspect that this training is more likely to be used at a strategic, regional level than in the day-to-day life of the average simple church.) It is beyond the scope of this book to discuss how leaders of simple churches are raised up and trained in an ongoing fashion. We highly recommend Neil Cole's excellent book *Organic Leadership* for a discussion of this.

The following table is a comparison of leadership styles. The table consists of generalizations, which are always somewhat risky. It is not meant to be a blanket condemnation of old-style leaders—after all, many of us have been there ourselves, and we were living for God at the time. Many legacy church leaders are humble servants of God. But the system does make a difference. Church structure plays a role because it takes an "eagle" to lead and excel within most traditional church structures that are seeking to increase in size; but doves can lead simple churches.

NEW TESTAMENT LEADERSHIP

New Testament leadership is "flat," or nonhierarchical. Of the fourteen times that the New Testament uses the Greek word *poimen* (pastor/shepherd) as a noun, only one refers to a function in the church. The rest refer to Jesus. And leadership in the New Testament is always shared, a plurality or team working together.

The Bible does talk about appointing elders and deacons, and some people feel that in time, each individual house church should be overseen by an elder, someone who watches over those in his or her care. Others think that it is more likely that New Testament leadership—in the form of recognizing "elders"—happened within a region or city, rather than within each individual house church.[3]

Because the Scripture is not totally clear on this subject, we try not to be dogmatic about the way that leadership is established. What is clear is that we desperately need spiritual mothers and fathers to help provide stability to the simple churches and to care for the people within each group. The titles are not important; the function is.

Conventional Paradigm	Simple Paradigm
One man dominant in leadership	Jesus as head of the body working through many *(Colossians 1:18)*
Eagles	Doves *(1 Thessalonians 2:7)*
Hierarchical	Flat *(Matthew 20:25-28)*
Based on charisma	Based on character *(1 Timothy 3:1-13)*
Training in academic institutions	Trained by the Holy Spirit in real time *(2 Corinthians 11:22-29)*
CEO—keeps the programs running and the customers satisfied	Weeping father, longing for his son to overtake him *(1 Thessalonians 2:7-12)*
Manages programs and processes	Serves others as necessary *(Matthew 20:26-27; 2 Corinthians 4:5)*
"You carry my suitcase"	"I'll carry your suitcase" *(2 Corinthians 12:15)*
Visible on the stage	One of the crowd *(Ephesians 2:20)*
Superstar—larger than life	Ordinary—given to death *(John 15:13; 2 Corinthians 4:7-12; Galatians 2:20)*
Leader's vision that counts	Equips and releases others for their vision *(Ephesians 4:12)*
Showcases own gifts/talents	Equips others to minister *(Ephesians 4:11-12)*
Authority is positional	Spiritual authority based on relationship with Father *(John 5:19; 8:28)*

Centralized power, authority, control	Power and authority are decentralized and delegated *(1 Corinthians 3:5-9)*
Builds an empire	Builds the Kingdom *(Ephesians 4:11-12)*
Raises bar on leadership	Lowers bar on leadership *(Romans 16)*
Hard to multiply	Easy to multiply *(Acts 16:5)*
Maintains control	"Out of control"—control given to Holy Spirit *(John 16:13)*
Success measured by numbers, dollars, and real estate	Success based on obedience and faithfulness *(Acts 5:29; 2 Timothy 2:2)*
"How high can I fly?"	"How low can I go?" *(1 Corinthians 4:10-13; 2 Corinthians 12:9)*
Looking for earthly success and human respect	Looking for eternal rewards *(Philippians 2:5-8; 3:7-9)*
Ignores the weaker	Seeks and serves the weak *(1 Corinthians 12:22-24)*
Alpha male	Male and female *(Romans 16)*
Anoints a successor	Raises many sons and daughters *(2 Timothy 1:2; Titus 1:4; Philemon 1:10)*
Professional providing expertise	Everyone adds value *(1 Corinthians 12)*

Church leadership goes beyond the context of the local church, as we see in the ministries of Paul and others, such as the council of Jerusalem (Acts 15). And in the church today we see the Lord still at work producing apostles, prophets, evangelists, pastors, and teachers, just as He did in Ephesians.[4]

The New Testament tells us that the church is built on the foundation of apostles and prophets. Foundations are unseen, without prestige or status, yet without them a building would collapse. Paul had this to say about apostles:

> *For I think that God has displayed us, the apostles, last, as men condemned to death; for we have been made a spectacle to the world, both to angels and to men. We are fools for Christ's sake, but you are wise in Christ! We are weak, but you are strong! You are distinguished, but we are dishonored! To the present hour we both hunger and thirst, and we are poorly clothed, and beaten, and homeless. And we labor, working with our own hands. Being reviled, we bless; being persecuted, we endure; being defamed, we entreat. We have been made as the filth of the world, the offscouring of all things until now.*
> — I CORINTHIANS 4:9-13

Who wants to sign up to be an apostle?

The apostle Paul, writing to the church at Corinth, comments,

> *Even if you had ten thousand others to teach you about Christ, you have only one spiritual father. For I became your father in Christ Jesus when I preached the Good News to you.*
> — I CORINTHIANS 4:15, NLT

Paul "fathered" the church at Corinth and was naturally viewed by the Corinthians as an apostle. Obviously not everyone who has given a word in prophecy is a prophet, and not everyone who has planted a church is an apostle. However, some *are* called as apostles and others as prophets. This is biblical, and it is a gift of the ascended Jesus to His church (Ephesians 4:8-12).

In 1 Corinthians 12:28, Paul apparently gives a hierarchical list of ministries—"first apostles, second prophets, third teachers" and so on. Does this mean that apostles are the top dogs in the church? No. Paul's description is better suited to the way we build a house. First you need an architect, then someone to pour the foundation, and then someone to do the framing, etc. Apostles are those who are sent out—the word literally means "sent one"—to found a church. Prophets are needed to provide vision for that church. And the teachers provide an accurate understanding of the things of God. Each one plays a different role.

In Acts, we see teams of apostles going on missionary trips. For example, Paul and Barnabas, originally teachers and/or prophets, were sent out as apostles on their first missionary trip (Acts 13:1-4; 14:4). Then we see Paul and Silas (Acts 15:40), and later still, Paul has gathered a team of several men around him (Acts 20:4). No doubt he is teaching them the principles of church planting. Similarly, Agabus, a prophet, ministers with a team of other prophets (Acts 11:27-28).

CREATING DOVES FROM EAGLES

The simple church movement has surfaced from under the radar, and its apparent success puts it in a position of vulnerability. If leaders emerge who are "eagles" with the old paradigm of leadership—and none of us are immune to the temptation of power and control—the movement will soon revert to being just another denomination serving to further divide the body of Christ (1 Corinthians 1:10-13). It will only be by God's grace that we stay on track.

When we first moved to this country we had nine years of God's training school. We would never have chosen that path, but we know that it prepared us for what we are now involved in. We often hear of people who are going through great hardship and suffering of various kinds—the pain of financial difficulties, relational breakups, health issues, emotional challenges. And we think to ourselves, *Is this God at work creating doves out of eagles? Are they learning to die to themselves in His wilderness school? Is God preparing more leaders for His Kingdom?*

18

UNITY IN DIVERSITY

CENTURIES BEFORE THE church came into existence, the prophet Joel foresaw a day when there would be no racial or sexual inequalities among God's people. He predicted that God would pour out His Spirit on all flesh—whether male or female, slave or free.

> *"And it shall be in the last days," God says, "that I will pour forth of My Spirit on all mankind; and your sons and your daughters shall prophesy, and your young men shall see visions, and your old men shall dream dreams; even on my bondslaves, both men and women, I will in those days pour forth of My Spirit. And they shall prophesy."*
> —ACTS 2:17-18, NASB

Joel knew that God was not going to pour out His Spirit solely on the Jews, but on all humanity. Men and women across the nations would move under the power of the Spirit to spread the Good News of the Kingdom. When Peter quoted these words in Acts 2, he was living in an era when slavery was commonplace and women were regarded as mere possessions. Over the centuries, we have seen some of these inequities erode, and we can only hope that the church is now moving into a time when, as Galatians 3:28 says, "There is neither Jew nor Greek, there is neither slave nor free, there is neither male nor female; for you are all one in Christ Jesus."

ETHNIC DIVERSITY IN THE CHURCH

It's been said that the most segregated hour in America occurs on Sunday mornings when people of different ethnic backgrounds go to their own churches.[1] Yet we pray, "Your Kingdom come. Your will be done on earth as it is in heaven" (Matthew 6:10). And God has given us a picture of what heaven will be like as we read Revelation's description of a huge crowd gathered around the throne to worship God.

> *After these things I looked, and behold, a great multitude which no one could number, of all nations, tribes, peoples, and tongues, standing before the throne and before the Lamb, clothed with white robes, with palm branches in their hands.*
> —REVELATION 7:9

It's no secret that incredible injustices have been perpetrated on people of different races in this country. Even today, prejudice continues to run rampant, and discrimination can be seen in many forms: social, financial, judicial, and political. Although some politicians have tried to correct these inequities, the church has done little to redress the imbalance.

A friend of ours who is African American was invited to be the "black representative" for his denomination and was placed in a church to work as an associate minister. Some of the members of the congregation rejected the idea of having a black man in a leadership position and boycotted the church both physically and financially. When the wealthier people left the church, the denominational leadership gave in to the protesters and asked this man to leave so the church could return to business as usual.

On another occasion, this same man was asked to speak at the men's dinner of a church. Some of the men refused to attend the dinner, calling it "The Last Supper" because a black man was speaking.

Most Christians claim to be color-blind. They would say that in Jesus, we are all equal, and since color does not matter to Him, neither does it matter to them. This is a good start. But our African American brothers and sisters will tell you that this is not what they are looking for. They would rather the body of Christ actively welcome diversity, enjoy our ethnic differences, and rejoice in the variety of cultures represented. The church is not complete unless we recognize, embrace, and include every tribe and tongue and nation.

What are we in simple church going to do about diversity? National studies show that African Americans are twice as likely to be involved in simple church as the rest of the population.[2] Simple church is also a perfect fit for the strong family-based culture of the Hispanic population. We can choose to go out of our way to make sure that people of other cultures are included at every level of what goes on in simple church—both in leadership and in our gatherings.

True diversity within the church will not be without its challenges—like music. African Americans often find the music of the Anglo world to be relatively bland compared to the rhythm and vigor their culture loves. A black friend of ours recently attended a meeting where white musicians were leading a predominantly black congregation in worship. He said the time was uninspired until someone from the back of the room started to sing the well-known spiritual "Hallelujah." Something in the atmosphere changed, he said, and the whole congregation began to sing unreservedly. He described it as "pressing through to find the music of heaven."

In the same way, we may need to press through to find the culture of heaven in various different areas—but it will be worth any struggle we go through.

We have much to learn from other cultures. Thomas Wynn and Richard Fowlkes, African American friends of ours, were recently given an opportunity for prominence, but in response they voluntarily chose service. In their own network of simple churches, they care for one another in practical ways, modeling New Testament principles of selfless servanthood. Richard even gives up several hours each day to drive some of the young men in their community to work because they do not have transportation.

We love the way Thomas demonstrates New Testament leadership. A tall man, he stands over someone sitting in a chair and says, "This is how leadership in the church used to be: I am over you. You will fulfill my vision." But then he kneels down so that he is looking at the person face-to-face and says, "But this is how it is in simple church. We are on the same level. You get to know me. You see how I lead my life. You see how I interact with my wife and kids. And if you like what you see, you ask me to lead you."

He continues, "And now I go to the highest point in the room." Then he kneels low and holds that person's feet. "From now on, I am here to serve you and the vision God has given you. All my resources are available to you. What part of me do you need to stand on in order to reach your full potential in Christ? If you see me even reaching as high as your ankles, you let me know and I will get low again." He explains to that person that after a while he or she will be healed and fulfilled. To demonstrate this he asks the person to stand with his or her hands raised high in praise to God.

"Now how will you lead someone else? Go to the highest place in the room . . ." Then he leads that person to kneel at someone else's feet.

What a powerful lesson! For the sake of the gospel, these Christians have willingly embraced something they fought against for centuries: slavery. If only the whole body of Christ could learn from this example!

While Christians may understand the need to stand up for justice and equality for all people, we need to take it one step further and genuinely embrace every race. Will this simple church movement rise up to the challenge? Will we stand up for heaven's culture of diversity? Do we care enough to make a difference?

THE ROLE OF WOMEN IN THE KINGDOM OF GOD

The term *hemiplegic* is used by those in the medical profession to describe paralysis on one side of the body (such as occurs after a stroke). In the same way, the body of Christ in the Western world can be described as hemiplegic. Half the body of Christ is, for the most part, not functioning because usually the women are left out of strategic roles. Even within the simple church context in the West, the majority of leaders are male.

Traditionally, in many Bible-believing evangelical churches, women have not been in leadership. Women may run the Sunday school or a prayer ministry, but when it comes to leading the church as a whole, or being in a position that might give direction to the body of Christ, with some notable exceptions, women are usually not included, because certain Scriptures apparently limit their role. Currently among all of the Protestant senior pastors in America, just 9 percent are female: in addition, there are no women priests in the Catholic church.[3]

Down through the years, women in the church have been kept out of leadership for a number of different reasons:

- "Of course under God, we are all equal; it is just that we have different roles." (This sounds remarkably like George Orwell's famous dictum from *Animal Farm*: "All animals are equal, but some animals are more equal than others.")
- "Women can lead—they do it by exerting influence through their husbands."
- "God does use women, but only when He cannot find a man for the job."

The belief that Scripture forbids women from teaching or leading within the church has led to some ludicrous situations. Chinese Christian author and church leader Watchman Nee learned a great deal from two gifted women preachers, but because they were not allowed to teach men, on at least one occasion, a large white sheet was hung across the hall for the men to sit behind while they listened to the message being preached by the women.[4]

The movement of churches we were involved with in the United Kingdom initially subscribed to this philosophy. During the 1970s, we were going through a period of revival, and God was doing exciting and extraordinary things all over the country. But Felicity had to remain at home while Tony attended men's leadership weekends. He always came back fired up and abundantly blessed, while she had been at home, coping with kids and diapers. It was not that Felicity minded being at home with the family—she loved that and was delighted Tony had met with the Lord—but she still felt excluded from the real movement of the Spirit, simply because of her gender.[5]

God clearly gifts both men and women with a passion for hearing His voice and then imparting that message to the body of Christ. But too often, women are told they can only exert influence through their husbands.

Many women long to be where the real action is, which in many cases is in the men's meetings. God often gives women the same desire as men to be involved in Kingdom strategy. That might not necessarily include public leadership, but it may mean wanting to be more involved with the planning and strategic thinking. And the fact that gender prevents this often leads to a deep and intense sadness and disappointment.

Felicity spent many hours in tears, year after year, feeling frustrated that she was somehow left out of the best that God was doing, simply because of her gender. She asked the Lord again and again why she had these desires to serve Him in this way. Had He given them to her, or were they just worldly, self-ish ambition? And if He had given them, couldn't He take them away so that she could be content to just sit on the sidelines like she was supposed to?

The frustration and helplessness felt by women is very similar to that felt by people who are discriminated against in other areas, like race and social class.

However, in Felicity's situation, she wanted more than anything else for the Kingdom to be extended, and if this meant she was to take a backseat, that was what she would do. If the Scriptures really said that women were not to be involved, then she was willing to submit.

When we moved to America, we eventually became involved in simple church. And in this move of God, there is no discrimination against women in leadership. Today in the simple church movement, women are fully functioning within the body of Christ. Some are starting churches; some are acting as catalysts for regional networks; others are teaching. There are women who are apostles and others who move prophetically. There are no barriers because of their gender.

Jesus died to bring us liberty, not captivity. The whole trend of the Bible, especially the New Testament, is toward freedom and emancipation. Jesus epitomized this in His own attitude toward women, treating them as equals. Some of His most important theological conversations were with women, like Martha and the woman at the well. Women supported Him in ministry and stayed with Him even as He died. A woman anointed Him for burial, and the very first person He chose to show Himself to after His resurrection was Mary Magdalene.

Throughout the New Testament, women served as beloved coworkers. Of the twenty-one specific people mentioned in Romans 16, seven were women, one of whom (Junia) was a leading apostle.[6]

Christians have often been in the forefront when it comes to issues of emancipation. It was Christians like William Wilberforce and Harriet Beecher Stowe who fought for the abolition of slavery.

But frequently, God uses society to speak prophetically to the church. Women are far more valued in today's society than they have ever been before. How slow the church has been to even notice what God has allowed to happen in the world around us!

In Galatians 3:28, we see that there is neither Jew nor Greek, slave nor free, male nor female; all are one in Christ. It is past time for women's equality. This is not a militant feminism but merely the need for women to be recognized as equal in value and fully able to play a strategic role in the church.

In 1983, we had the privilege of spending time with David (Paul) Yonggi Cho, pastor of what was then the largest church in the world. One of the most insightful things Dr. Cho said that day was this: "You people in the West will never see a move of God until you use your women. Women have been key to what has happened in Korea."

God is already using women in extraordinary ways in countries all over the world. In China, women and teenagers spread the gospel during the darkest days of Mao's persecution, when the men were all imprisoned. In countries like India, many women are starting churches. One friend of ours, a home-maker in her sixties, has trained over eight thousand women, and as a result, more than six thousand churches have been started. Another American friend, a young woman in her thir-ties, currently works in an area of rural India. In the several years that she has been there, she has seen over seven hundred churches start.

In Mozambique, Heidi Baker is a true example of a modern-day female apostle. With her husband, Rolland, she has wit-nessed the start of ten thousand plus churches, mostly in Mozambique and the surrounding countries of Africa.[7]

Since the Holy Spirit (the author of Scripture) does not go against scriptural principles, it's important to understand some of the more difficult passages in the Bible that seem to indicate that women have a lesser role to play.

Let's take one of the problem passages as an example. At first glance, 1 Corinthians 14:34-35 seems perfectly clear: women are to remain silent in church.

> *Let your women keep silent in the churches, for they are not permitted to speak; but they are to be submissive, as the law also says. And if they want to learn something, let them ask their own husbands at home, for it is shameful for women to speak in church.*

The first indication of a problem, however, is that nowhere in the law does it say that women are to be submissive. We know from 1 Corinthians 11 that women can speak in church, since they are told to pray and prophesy with their heads covered.

To really understand this passage's meaning, we need to look at it within its context. First Corinthians 7:1 begins with these words: "Regarding the questions you asked in your letter . . ." (NLT). It is obvious that Paul is addressing various topics, apparently in answer to questions the Corinthians posed to him in an earlier letter.

The word meaning "to be silent" (*sigao*) is used three times in 1 Corinthians 14, presumably in response to problems raised by the church in one of their letters. In verse 28, it is used in reference to people speaking in tongues when there is no one present to interpret. Paul tells them to be silent (*sigao*) and to speak to themselves and God. In verse 30, Paul is addressing the dilemma that occurs when more than one person has a prophecy at the same time. He says the first one to prophesy should hold his peace (*sigao*).

The difficulty we have in understanding verse 34, where the term is used in reference to women speaking in church, is that the problem or question is not first discussed. Maybe Paul felt it was self-evident from the answer he gave. We can assume that some women were being disruptive by asking questions in the middle of the meetings, and Paul told them to be quiet (*sigao*) and ask their husbands at home.

In neither of the first two situations would anyone presume the silence was to be permanent and in every meeting. The directive was only for a certain set of circumstances. Yet verse 34 has been used to keep women silent in church for centuries. There are some churches even today that literally forbid women to speak (even to pray aloud) in their services.

Whenever we address this subject, women always come to

us afterward in tears. The vast majority have been hurt in some way by the attitude of the church toward women.

Recently we have seen deep repentance by some of the men in leadership within the simple church movement over the way women have been treated down through the centuries. These have been times of healing, especially when they go on to validate women by declaring their freedom to do anything the Lord calls them to.

Of course, not every woman is called to a leadership role (just as not all men are called to leadership). Many are more than content to look after their homes and families, and that's fine—if it is what God is calling them to. For most women, there needs to be a season when children are their primary focus.

For many women, however, the barriers against moving out freely into strategic leadership roles are still there—even if the obstacles are primarily in our own minds. We have a dog, a chocolate Labrador wannabe, named Sugar. She is pure mutt, but the Lab part of her loves to wander. Our home has a fence around it with an automatic gate. Sugar used to lie in wait for a car to exit, and then, just as the gate was almost closed again, she would make her bid for freedom. For various reasons, we decided the time had come to stop her from going AWOL. So we installed an invisible fence across the driveway in front of the gate. An invisible fence works because the dog receives a jolt of electricity from a battery on its collar if it crosses a certain line.

Sugar is not normally a very fast learner, but it only took a couple of, shall we say, shocking experiences before she learned not to go out of the gate. From that time on, she would sit in the driveway, looking longingly at the open gate, without ever attempting to cross the line. Long after the battery in her collar had totally died, she would not go out the gate. She had become conditioned to stay within her boundaries.

Those of us who are women have become conditioned to gender-related boundaries. Even though these barriers are no longer in existence, we still do not feel free to exercise the liberty we have in Christ. As Christian women, we need to ask God for vision and courage to go beyond the limits of church convention and do all He would have us do.

Men also have a role to play in freeing women into their destiny. Tony is a very gifted communicator, but he came to realize that the only time Felicity would speak out was when he kept quiet. For many husbands, the only way they can help their wives to take their rightful place as equal ministers within the Kingdom is to willingly stand down and joyfully promote their wives' gifts. At first, it might seem that the men of the church could have done the job far better than the women are doing. But that's only because they have had far more practice. In the long run, allowing women to exercise their gifts will make for a much fuller expression of the body of Christ.

We have seen how many men have led down through the centuries—through rivalry and competition, position grabbing and control, ego promoting, and a quest for the limelight. Women can learn from this. As we have opportunity to take strategic positions, let's deliberately opt for the path of humility and service.

As women, we are now faced with some choices. We can decide that the church owes us some status, that we deserve position and authority, and that we have the right to take what is legitimately ours. Or we can willingly choose to lay down our rights and to serve with humility in whatever God is doing. We have the advantage of centuries of learning how to serve and lay down our lives for others. The body of Christ will be richer as we willingly embrace that calling, moving ahead into whatever He would have us do.

TRUTH HAS TWO WINGS

There is a great diversity in theological opinion within the simple church movement. Currently we seem to span the whole spectrum of conventional Christian beliefs. And so far, everyone seems content to embrace a diversity of viewpoints without any sign of division. But history tells us this may not always prove true. We may be forced to a choice. Are we going to stand together in unity despite our theological differences, or will we allow them to divide us? Jesus' longest recorded prayer was that His people would be one (John 17).

Tony loves to debate. In school, he delighted in tying others up with words, especially in the public forum of a classroom debate. But life, and especially the Christian life, is not a debate but a journey. It is not a destination at which we have arrived so much as a pathway on which we are just embarking. We like to think that we know all of the answers, but in reality, the more we learn, the more we realize that there are not only others who know more but others who see things differently.

When we were pioneering a church in the East End of London, we used to have "hot potato" evenings. (In England, a "hot potato" is a topic too hot to handle.) We looked at subjects like militarism and pacifism, Calvinism and Arminianism, women in ministry and women keeping silent in the church. One evening a mock fight was staged in the middle of a debate on eschatology (issues surrounding the second coming of

Christ). Two church leaders were debating the issue. Unknown to anyone else, it had been arranged for another well-known leader in the church to be in the audience and to stand up and challenge what was being shared. He and one of the debaters were to get into an argument and the one in the congregation would finally shout, "If this is what you really believe then I'm leaving the church!" and storm out of the room. All went according to plan. Everyone watching was aghast, some even in tears. Eventually they stopped and explained that it was just a "live" demonstration of how silly it is to divide on such relatively inconsequential issues. There is far more that unites us than divides us.

Why is it that when it comes to theological issues, we're all so sure that we are correct and that everyone else needs to agree with us? On virtually any issue we choose to explore, we can find equally sincere and godly people who disagree with us. Shouldn't this give us some cause for caution and humility?

At the House2House National Conference some years ago, Rolland Baker, a well-known Pentecostal missionary from Mozambique, shared some of his experiences of the power of God in action. Many were touched by the Lord, including by what some considered to be very strange manifestations of God—such things as "holy laughter," being "slain in the spirit," and speaking in tongues. For the 50 percent or more at the conference who had no previous exposure to these things, this raised many questions that we felt should be addressed before the whole conference. In the main session that evening, with everyone present, we set up something along the lines of our old British "hot potato" nights. Kent Smith, a respected academic from Abilene Christian University, asked Neil Cole (from a

Grace Brethren/noncharismatic background) and Tony (from an openly charismatic background) some questions about the things that were going on. What an interesting and healing time this was for all involved. It dissolved any tension that might have arisen. Neil, the noncharismatic, made it very plain that all we were seeing had clear biblical and historical precedent, while Tony talked about the fact that any experience of the gifts or manifestations of the Holy Spirit without the character to match was like "a noisy gong or a clanging cymbal" (1 Corinthians 13:1, NLT).

Much in our experience of God has balance and counterbalance. He chose us (Romans 8:29), but we also chose Him (John 1:12). Nothing can separate us from the love of God (Romans 8:39), but we can clearly choose to separate from Him (Hebrews 10:26). No one can say Jesus is Lord except by the Holy Spirit (1 Corinthians 12:3), yet Paul can ask the believers in Ephesus, "Did you receive the Holy Spirit when you believed?" (Acts 19:2, NASB).

Truth often has two wings.[8] Part of maturity is learning to live with the tension. "'My thoughts are nothing like your thoughts,' says the Lord. 'And my ways are far beyond anything you could imagine'" (Isaiah 55:8, NLT). God is not bound by our logic or by what we can understand.

Many of the concepts we struggle with fall into this category. We are saved by grace through faith, and it is a gift of God (Ephesians 2:8, NASB), yet we "work out [our] own salvation with fear and trembling" (Philippians 2:12, but notice also verse 13: "For it is God who works in you"). We have seen beliefs about law and grace separate Christians. We have seen obligation put on Christians to follow the law, and we have heard loving grace wooing a similar response. Which emphasis is right? How do we decide on issues like these, where we may be able to argue equally passionately and biblically on differing sides of the same question?

Part of the answer must be that we learn to embrace differences. We rejoice in the diverse insights in the body of Christ. We value those who see things from another perspective, and we deliberately look for opportunities to learn from them. We learn to be passionate about what we believe and experience of the goodness of God, even while acknowledging that God may choose to work very differently in others.

Church history is littered with denominations and churches that arose because Christians disagreed over theological minutiae. We pray that we, as a movement, will not allow ourselves to be divided over our differing persuasions but instead strive for unity in Christ.

19

KINGDOM FINANCES

You can learn a lot about any movement by the way its members handle the issue of finances. Jesus said that one cannot serve God and money. Nowhere is the necessity of a changed heart or way of thinking more clearly seen than in the way churches and Christians handle their finances.

In the Sermon on the Mount, Jesus calls us to "seek first the kingdom of God and His righteousness" (Matthew 6:33). We have always tried to live full-time for the Lord, whether we were working in the medical profession, in the business world, or in paid ministry positions. Actually we believe there is no difference between sacred and secular. When we were working in the medical field, we brought our faith to bear on our professional lives by leading our patients to the Lord or praying for their various needs. It was a great open door for the Kingdom. Since being in business, we have seen the same open doors to lead business colleagues to Christ.

LIVING BY FAITH

We've always viewed our paying jobs as a means for God to financially provide for our calling to ministry. And during the times that we weren't receiving regular paychecks, we continued to learn the reality of "living by faith."

We found our four years of "living by faith" to be quite an experience. We had three young kids at the time, along with a mortgage and all the usual bills that a young family has to pay. We never knew how we were going to survive, but we always attempted to follow the Holy Spirit's lead. And God always provided. We remember one time when He challenged us to give away our last five dollars. Within a few hours of our doing so, someone had given us a gift of two hundred dollars! Sometimes sacks of groceries were left on our doorstep; sometimes envelopes of money would show up in our mailbox. And our money always seemed to stretch further than usual. We kept a wonderful steak meal in our freezer because if we ever ran out of food, we planned to go out with a bang by eating steak as our "last supper." But the Lord never once let us down, so eventually we just ate the steak anyway.

Just prior to our move to America, Tony was working in a ministry to doctors and others in the caring professions. We naively assumed that we would continue this work in the United States and that it would only take a short while before we would be earning a salary from it as we had in the United Kingdom. We were wrong!

Once we were in the United States, the ministry went down like a lead balloon. Soon finances became a major problem. We had no ministry to support us, and as we were not licensed to practice medicine in the United States, we were unemployable. So in order to make ends meet, we took on menial jobs. Tony did a variety of things, including door-to-door sales and running a flea market booth. Not the kind of thing you would imagine a distinguished physician (or minister) resorting to. But this work did develop character—nine years' worth of character.

Toward the latter part of this time, we started asking God that He would give us the "power to get wealth, that He may establish His covenant which He swore to your fathers as it is this day" (Deuteronomy 8:18). We asked Him for creative ideas, and He responded by giving us the idea to start the business that today supports us and enables us to take much time directly for Kingdom-related activity. Throughout this journey we have been learning that all work is God's work, and whatever the Holy Spirit is leading us to do at any given time is the way that we "seek first the kingdom of God and His righteousness" (Matthew 6:33).

HEALING PAST WRONGS

In the West, the simple church movement is still in its early stages and immature in many ways, especially in the area of finances. Part of the challenge we face is that Christians have suffered serious financial abuse by the church in the past. We have all heard tales of people being told that they can get out of debt if they give to the Lord (and more specifically to the minister who is speaking). These teachings are based on half-truths that tragically put people in bondage. The secular media tells stories of ministers living in opulent multimillion-dollar homes and driving large new luxury cars while those they minister to are barely making ends meet. According to Todd Johnson, studies show that billions (that's right, with a *b*) of dollars every year are misappropriated by churches, ministries, and those who have been entrusted with looking after the money donated.[1] It appears that Judas is still often in charge of the purse. Add to this the multiplied millions that are spent on ornate new buildings, programs, and additional staff members. It is easy to see why people might become cynical.

We've seen many come into the simple church movement from more traditional settings who are wounded and damaged in this area. They are wary of any instruction at all as it relates to the financial arena. As a result, many simple churches rarely mention giving, and most people choose to give to other ministries or projects rather than through a coordinated effort of their churches. Or worse yet, their giving dwindles or dries up altogether.

This is probably a temporary phase during which the Holy Spirit is bringing healing to people. The Bible is clear in its teaching on generous giving. Charity has always been a component of the life and ministry of every committed Christian. But Jesus and the New Testament writers made it clear that this flows out of a willing heart, rather than from a sense of grudging compulsion.

CORPORATE GIVING

If simple churches or networks of churches were to seek the Lord and gain vision for giving corporately to what He tells them to, they would probably be able to accomplish much more in Kingdom terms. The answer does not lie in ignoring the subject but rather in seeing people healed and establishing solid financial principles in their lives. However, this needs to be done with sensitivity.

A great example of simple churches sensitively handling finances could be seen after the 2007 elections in Kenya. Hundreds in that nation were killed and hundreds of thousands made homeless due to ethnic rivalries following the elections. We received an e-mail from a leader of a small network of simple churches there, describing the violence. Several of the young girls in that church had been raped multiple times, and many people were dead. In fact, his group alone had conducted ten funerals within one week. Earlier in 2007, a team of simple church people from the States had visited Kenya to encourage the growth of simple churches. Upon hearing the news of these atrocities, they quickly set up a Web site (http://www .simplechurchescare.com) to provide a way for people to give financially to the people of this needy country. Within a few days, several thousand dollars had been given for food, blankets, medicine, and mosquito nets. The impact of this gift in the refugee camps was profound.

BIBLICAL FINANCIAL PRINCIPLES

Let's look in more detail at the subject of money. As always, the Bible provides principles to live by. Jesus spoke frequently about money. Many of His parables related to finances within the Kingdom, and some of His most challenging teaching was on this topic. Jesus clearly emphasized that rather than placing our security in personal wealth or possessions, we should trust God to supply our needs. We can either serve God or mammon (money), but we cannot serve both! As Wolfgang Simson likes to say, "You can choose to live by faith or by calculation."[2]

This is not to ignore New Testament teaching that we should work with our hands to support our families (1 Thessalonians 4:11-12), but rather we need to understand the biblical emphasis on developing a total trust in the Lord.

In this country, many people struggle with personal finances that are in disarray. They use their credit cards unwisely and live beyond their means, often spending their hard-earned money on things that are nonessential. Very few people have received training in the management of family finances either from their parents, the education system, or the church. Sadly the financial condition of people in the church is often no different than of those outside the church.[3]

The Bible is filled with sound financial principles. John Wesley, a man God used to bring revival to England, summed up his understanding of what the Bible teaches about money this way: "Gain all you can, save all you can, and give all you can."[4] We are to work hard, live simply, and give all we can to the Kingdom.[5]

Many excellent resources have been produced on the topic of family finances, including those from Crown Financial Ministries,[6] David Mallonee's Concepts in Stewardship,[7] and Dave Ramsey's Financial Peace University.[8] Simple churches could greatly benefit from these resources.

We need to take seriously Jesus' statement in Luke 16:11 (NLT): "And if you are untrustworthy about worldly wealth, who will trust you with the true riches of heaven?" What might happen if we, the people who make up this simple church movement, became faithful in the handling of our personal finances?

One of the biggest advantages of simple churches is that they do not have high overheads. Usually there are no facilities to pay for and no salaries to provide. This leaves plenty of money to give away to mission projects or those in need. Many of the simple churches we know give away as much as 85 percent of what comes in. At the Association of Home Churches in Killeen, Texas, God has led all the leaders there to be bivocational. Over the past twelve years, this network of simple churches has given over a million dollars to benevolence and mission organizations.

The New Testament clearly describes those in the church taking care of those in need.

> *Nor was there anyone among them who lacked; for all who were possessors of lands or houses sold them, and brought the proceeds of the things that were sold, and laid them at the apostles' feet; and they distributed to each as anyone had need.*
>
> —ACTS 4:34-35

People were encouraged to first take care of their own family members, and then the church helped the true widows (1 Timothy 5:3-16). And this giving was not limited to the local context. For example, following Agabus's prophecy of a famine, the disciples in Antioch (part of Asia Minor) collected money for the believers in Judea (part of Israel) (Acts 11:28-30).

We know of many situations where caring for one another is worked out in practical ways. Several times, the churches we are involved with have helped those who cannot afford to pay for a car repair or who are in danger of losing their electricity because of an unpaid bill.

SUPPORTING THOSE IN FULL-TIME MINISTRY

Most traditional churches provide support for those in full-time ministry. First Corinthians 9 shows clearly that those who preach the gospel can live by the gospel (see verse 14). Jesus Himself was supported by others, particularly a group of women. Jesus often stayed in people's homes and they provided Him with food.

How do we apply these principles in a simple church context? Although this is predominantly a movement of laypeople, there is clearly a place for those who are in full-time ministry, those who because of extensive travel or other opportunities to serve the body are unable to have a job to support themselves. For the most part, these people are currently receiving funds from more traditional means—foundations, denominations, mission organizations, and so on. For some, "full-time" ministry is only possible because their spouses willingly support them. As the simple church movement matures, it should be able to support its own people whom the Lord calls. We should be eager, like the believers in 2 Corinthians 9:2, to be very generous to those who serve the body of Christ.

However, although he clearly spells out the principle that those who travel to preach the gospel should be supported by those who are benefiting from it (1 Corinthians 9:5-14), Paul goes on to say that he would rather die than exercise that privilege (1 Corinthians 9:15). Whenever he spent any reasonable length of time in one place, Paul worked to support himself (Acts 18:3; 20:34-35). So what should we do? As always, when the Scriptures are not obvious in an area, the answer lies in finding out what God is saying to our specific situation. He is the one in charge of financing His Kingdom, and He can let us know which path He wants us to take. We have the mind of Christ (1 Corinthians 2:16).

What about those who have been in full-time ministry in a legacy church but have now been led into simple churches? How can they support themselves, especially if they don't appear qualified for other work?

Recently we've begun to hear stories about new ways that God is helping people to generate income, leading people into business ventures of various kinds and then blessing those businesses. Often it is only a year or so before these people are able to hire others to do the work, freeing themselves for greater service once again. But this time, they are funded by their businesses. (Those who are successful in business could help in this area by acting as coaches or creating new jobs.)

Other simple church members are entering into various other forms of employment. In 1 Timothy 3, one of the qualifications for leadership is that he or she be well thought of by the world. We earn credibility when we work to support ourselves. We also gain a new opportunity for connecting with a community in ways we have not known before. A good friend of ours returned from the mission field and eventually found work at his local Wal-Mart. He values the way this helps him relate to others. Others in the simple church movement are raising their own support just as if they were traveling to the foreign mission field. Finally, in some locations, God is leading networks of churches to help support qualified leaders once they have already proven themselves to be fruitful within the Kingdom.

We are all called to be kings and priests (1 Peter 2:9). There is no clergy/laity divide. We are all called to be "full time." The problem when leaders are paid is that, whether we like it or not, it re-creates the clergy/laity distinction.

In a recent House2House article entitled "Can It Be That Simple?" Bill Hoffman says,

> *The key is in listening to the heart of our Treasurer. Are we in a season of giving or receiving? Chances are we will each experience both seasons moving back and forth from one to another often throughout our lifetime. We need to have "ears to hear" our Treasurer. When it is time to give He will let us know and He will make certain the funds are there to obey His directive. When it is time to receive He will tell us to set aside our pride and accept His grace. There are wonderful blessings in each season. "Not that I am looking for a gift, but I am looking for what may be credited to your account. I have received full payment and even more; I am amply supplied. . . . And my God will meet all your needs according to his glorious riches in Christ Jesus"* (PHILIPPIANS 4:17-19, NIV).[9]

Could Kingdom finances be as simple as listening to God, doing what He says, and then trusting Him with the results? We believe so!

20

CHALLENGES TO
THE MOMENTUM

THE SIMPLE CHURCH movement is gaining momentum all the time. As thrilling as this is, we must stop and recognize that there are some inherent dangers in approaching the tipping point (the time at which an idea goes from being unknown to mainstream).[1]

Are we misleading people when we say that this work of God through simple churches could produce a movement that is as influential as the Reformation?

Outside visitors and ministries can often help a simple church see more clearly why it is running into difficulties. For that reason it is important to seek outside help or coaching from those with more experience if things do not seem to be going well.[2]

Simple church is not a feel-good, goosebumps movement. In a large congregation it is easy to think that everyone is doing okay, but the reality may be far from that. As people hop on the bandwagon of simple church, hoping that this time their problems with church will be solved, they tend to bring their baggage with them. In a small group, most people quickly let their guard down and everything becomes more real. For this reason problems are more likely to surface in simple churches.

While home-based fellowships will be fresh and exciting at first, as people trade the formal sermons for informal meals, they almost inevitably reach the point where they miss the programs that traditional church can offer. Simple church just can't compete with the professional quality of a large-scale worship event, the teaching, and of course, the kids' programs. Not only that, there is no one to hand over all the decision making and responsibility to—the whole body is involved.

Is it easy to become disillusioned? Of course. It is likely that we will soon receive reports that go something like this:

- "I tried house church for a year. I bought the T-shirt, read the books, and went to the conferences, but it wasn't for me."
- "It didn't work—and besides, there was nothing for my kids. I'm going back to my old church."

RECOGNIZE DEATH VALLEY

Wolfgang Simson says that when Christians transition from traditional church to simple church, they can see the mountaintop of simple church from the summit of the mountain of legacy church. It looks so close and so inviting they assume they can move directly from one mountaintop to another. What they do not see is the unavoidable Death Valley between the two.[3]

Leaving the mountaintop of legacy church involves dying to good things—the diversity of the programs, the professional teaching, the worship band, the full-time leadership. Some people refer to this process as a time of "detox." It takes time to get the old ways of doing things out of your system. It takes time to appreciate the informality of the 24-7 lifestyle of simple church. It takes time to truly understand at a gut level that a church gathering really can be as simple as a group of people hanging out in the Lord's presence, listening to God and to each other, and following His agenda for their time together.

This is not a sudden, painless death. It can be agonizingly slow, often in terms of years, and the temptation to bail out of the process can be overwhelming. Some simple churches fail because they do not press through Death Valley to the mountaintop on the other side.

"HONEY, I SHRUNK THE CHURCH!"

Church is not based on where we meet. However, we have found that most of the core values of the New Testament church are easier to foster within the more intimate environment of a home. One of the biggest mistakes a simple church can make is to merely swap the four walls of the church building for the four walls of the living room. If we're not careful, we aren't doing anything more than "shrinking the church," so that it fits within our living rooms.[4] We ask someone to lead the worship and another to teach. The lone guitarist does not get the chords right, and the teaching is far from intellect stretching. We cannot rely on a gifted leader to make all the decisions.

But this is not simple church. A true simple church gathering is just that—simple. We are a community of Jesus lovers with the belief that the Holy Spirit's agenda is more important than our own, and a willingness to press through to reach it. First Corinthians 14:26 (NIV) says this:

What then shall we say, brothers? When you come together, everyone has a hymn, or a word of instruction, a revelation, a tongue or an interpretation. All of these must be done for the strengthening of the church.

Once we have tasted this on a regular basis, nothing else will satisfy.

MISSIONAL DNA

Simple church is, above all, a change in DNA. It is a paradigm shift in how the church of Jesus Christ thinks and operates.

Neil Cole describes simple church DNA as:

- **Divine truth** (The revelation of God to mankind—based on the truths of God's Word and the person of Jesus)
- **Nurturing relationships** (Just as God is relational, so we humans are created with an intrinsic need for relationship.)
- **Apostolic mission** (We are sent out as God's representatives with His message to mankind.)[5]

If any of these are missing, a simple church will have challenges. The most likely of these core values to be absent is apostolic mission. If this is primarily a movement of people leaving the building to meet in small groups, then the only thing we have seen is transfer growth, not true Kingdom expansion.

If a simple church does not have a deliberate outward focus, sooner or later it will become stagnant. We need to seek the Lord and ask Him to give us inventive ideas for ways we can be His living body to the people He sends us to.

A great example of this comes from a network of simple churches called "Intentional Gatherings" that work with the homeless.

Aaron Snow writes:

Things are happening. This weekend we had an experience that encouraged us, broke our hearts, and gave us great hope all at the same time.

A strong relationship exists between our group and two people who have grown dear to our hearts over the past few months. We were challenged to love at a new level, and to take the next step in what it means to serve those in need. Last Monday, Robert and Laura called us from "their" pay phone. (Robert and Laura are homeless; they walk about a mile to the pay phone each week to call us.) We try to get together with them occasionally to eat, laugh, and get them any supplies they need. When they called this time, we made plans to pick them up on Saturday and spend the day with them.

Every Saturday morning at around 6:45 one of

our "gatherers" takes a group downtown to meet for what he calls the "Soul Café." Coffee is served to the homeless as they fill the streets after being sent out of the shelters for the day. This past Saturday in the parking lot of an old abandoned building there was no small crowd of people. About ten people from our network of organic churches spend a couple of hours hanging out with the homeless of Fort Worth. They all have different stories. Some are straight-up drunks. Some are drug addicts. Others lost their job ten years ago and can't seem to get a grip on life. They have no friends, no family, no home, and nothing but the clothes on their backs to their names. Physical, mental, and emotional needs are met on Saturday mornings.

After spending some time at the Soul Café, we usually head over to the woods to visit our friend Charlie, who is pushing seventy years of age. He's a sweet man. We spent some great time with Charlie; he laughed a lot. As we were leaving, a couple of us were saying our good-byes to Charlie. Here are Charlie's words to the four of us who remained:

"You know, I was thinking the other day after the last time you guys were here. I decided that you guys are like my grandchildren."

I immediately yelled for my friend Keri, who was on her way back to the car. She returned quickly, and I filled her in on what Charlie had just said. She looked at Charlie and said, "Charlie, I'll be your granddaughter!" For the rest of my life I will never forget the look on Charlie's face as his eyes filled with tears. Charlie, for the first time in a decade, has a family. He calls us his adopted grandkids. Charlie is no longer alone in the woods. He knows that his adopted grandkids love him.

The day had just begun. We made our way to the chain restaurant where we always meet Robert and Laura. They had everything they needed for the day. They hopped in the car, and I had to keep the windows rolled down on the way. Our friends had probably not showered in months. The odor was strong. We were excited that the Lord had allowed us to be a part of seeing this need met. We got to Keri's parents' house and the showering began.

Robert was hidden behind a long, thick beard, and until Saturday, I had never seen him without a cap on. We set out sandwich stuff on the table for lunch and spent time out on the back porch talking. When Laura came out from the shower, she was beautiful. Her hair was clean and brushed. She no longer had dirt staining her skin, and she smelled nice. She had a huge smile on her face.

Afterward, Robert hit the shower. When he was finished, my wife, Morgan, began cutting his hair. She must have cut five inches of hair from around his head; the top was bald. We all watched as Robert closed his eyes, smiled, and enjoyed the haircut—something he had not experienced in who knows how long.

We spend a lot of time with homeless people. They do not get touched very often. We make it a point to give out as many hugs as we can when we hang out with them. Morgan had the opportunity to give so much more than a hug. She touched, combed, brushed, ran her fingers through, and cut the hair of this homeless married couple. I had to ask myself how many girls I know who would do that. After cutting his hair, she went to work on his extremely long beard. Keri's dad, Bob, got a laugh from everyone when he returned from the garage with the hedge trimmers.

After Morgan cut the majority of the beard off, I began to carefully sculpt a sweet "trucker 'stache" out of the remaining beard on Robert's face. I had never been this close to Robert before. As I concentrated on shaving him, he just looked at me with big eyes and a huge smile. He was comfortable. I was comfortable. A trust had been developed between us. It rocked. He looked good!

Then it was Laura's turn. As Morgan began running her fingers through Laura's hair, Laura was in heaven on earth. She closed her eyes and relaxed as Morgan made her look even more beautiful on the outside than she already was.

The makeover was complete. Our friends were showered, dressed in clean clothes, fed, and floating on a cloud.

Robert and Laura hadn't been to the movies in over a year, so we took them to see one. I watched Robert through the entire movie, his face beaming as he leaned forward and crossed his arms on the chair in front of him. He rested his chin on his arms and stayed that way through the entire movie.

After the movie we asked them how they felt about us getting them a motel room for the night so they could sleep in a real bed under a roof. Robert's eyes watered, and he replied, "You guys really don't have to do that." We knew that, but we really wanted to do it. They graciously agreed, and we were on our way.

We found a place and got them settled into a room. We felt the need to share with Robert and Laura why we do what we do. We told them about Intentional Gatherings and what we do each week when we get together. We told them how we try to individually live out the gospel every day. We invited them to a cookout that we're having in a few weeks. They know that we will be singing, sharing, praying, and reading the Scriptures—and they are going to join us! Praise God! We told them that Christ has transformed our hearts and caused us to want to do nothing but extend grace and love toward those in need. We told them that we will love them no matter what they believe, and that our goal is not to convert them.

They were confused by our words. We continue to pray that the Lord would capture their souls and set them free. Please join us in that prayer.

We ordered a pizza to be delivered to their room, prayed over them, traded hugs, and headed home. We have an amazing vision of seeing Robert and Laura each week at our Intentional Gathering. In our minds we picture them sitting in the circle with us as we worship God. Robert is praying. . . .[6]

21

PITFALLS TO AVOID

It is not just the individual simple churches or networks that are facing challenges. This movement as a whole has some potentially challenging issues to overcome. If we are to move beyond transforming the church to the place of transforming our culture, we will need God's grace and guidance.

A BRILLIANT SUBSTITUTE

Some time ago, John Eldredge, author of *Wild at Heart* and *Waking the Dead*, was the speaker at a House2House national conference. Twice during his time with us, he publicly admonished us to "beware of the brilliant substitute." Those on the leadership team of House2House asked the Lord to help them better understand what this warning is about.

Imagine a megachurch starting "home churches" and

beaming the worship and the senior pastor's sermon into the living rooms of these groups via the Internet. Technically this is feasible, and it might even be a good way to start groups, but is this really the biblical model of "each one" bringing his or her part?

Imagine traditional churches just changing the name of their cell or home groups to "house church" and thinking they have the real thing. In their minds, the Sunday morning service is still "real church."

Imagine a program offering "Ten Steps to a Successful Simple Church: Follow these ten steps, and you, too, can have a genuine house church in your living room!" Since simple church is utterly dependent on the leading of the Holy Spirit and the participation of all of its members, it can never be reduced to a program.

In all actuality, we suspect that the "brilliant substitute" may be more subtle than any of these. Most people can see the dangers of the above examples, but if the substitute is truly brilliant, it has to have the potential of fooling any of us. We wonder if the brilliant substitute is church lived out of duty, doing the "right thing" rather than following the Holy Spirit out of passion for Jesus.

Our foundation for living in simple church is the ability to hear God's voice and then obey what He says.

A FASHIONABLE FAD

Another hazard we face is that of becoming fashionable, the latest phenomenon in church statistics, the trendy alternative to traditional church. There will always be people who hop onto the bandwagon because they want to be part of the latest thing, not because the Holy Spirit is leading them. But those who join the simple church movement without truly understanding and living out its DNA will soon find that what they have is only a pale substitute for the real thing.

A MOVEMENT WITHOUT MOMENTUM

At present, most simple churches across the nation are being started by people who have left legacy churches. It is a spontaneous, Spirit-inspired rebirth of church heart and structure, but it is still fueled primarily by transfer growth. As yet this still only represents a small advance in the Kingdom. And unless we make a deliberate choice to look outward, that is all it will become—a movement without momentum.

But we believe God is already changing that. Many, both in this country and around the world, are demonstrating to us that the Kingdom can grow quickly through prophetic evangelism[1] and supernatural encounters outside the four walls of the building. As the simple church movement learns to follow the Holy Spirit in the same way, praying for the needs of those we meet, we will find many people of peace who will open up their communities to the presence and power of Jesus.

We need to pray that what is happening will not just transform the church, but society as well. This will only happen as thousands and then tens of thousands in our cities are swept into the Kingdom. And it will involve all of us reaching out to those who come into our lives day by day.

A PEOPLE WITHOUT PASSION

According to sociologists, the widespread adoption of any idea requires going through a number of different phases. Innovators are adventurous, grabbing hold of an idea and running with it. These are the people with passion and fire who will go for something no matter what the cost. Early adopters check that the idea works, but then quickly join to support it, acting as role models for others who might follow later. They are usually the leaders in a movement. The majority of people follow after the innovators and early adopters. The idea has been proven to work, respectable leaders have gone ahead, and now they can follow. And they do, en masse. But they may lack the passion of those who have gone before because they have not had to pay the same price.

The simple church movement is somewhere between the early adoption and the majority phase. For many years, it was an underground movement, well below the radar screen of the Christian media. Those who were a part of it were dismissed as irrelevant, a tiny minority of believers with some off-the-wall ideas. In the last few years the concept has become respectable and many more people are getting involved. The danger is that those who are now joining don't have the same passion as the early adopters. There is little personal cost these days in starting a house church. And because of this, we run the risk of allowing an insipid, lukewarm Christianity to invade what, up until now, has been a zealous, committed band of Christ-followers.

Instead, we need to cry out to God on behalf of this movement, asking Him to infuse those who join it with His heart and purpose.

REVERTING TO TYPE

Some years ago, Bob Mumford gave a very interesting talk entitled "Frankenstein." In it he described how ideas often start with a group of people chatting around a kitchen table. The idea acquires a life of its own as it gains acceptance, crawls off the table, and eventually begins to control the people involved. If we're not careful, ideas can become "Frankensteins." Unless God gives us great wisdom, a few decades from now, these simple church movements will end up as a typical denomination.

We all have the tendency to revert to type. Typically what we have known in the past—that which is already familiar to us—becomes our default mode of handling things. But if we continue to do things as we have always done, the only thing we will accomplish will be to institutionalize the movement.

Obviously this movement needs leadership. God has given revelation about the character of this leadership, but as yet it is not totally clear how this will work itself out in practical terms. Over the past twenty years or more, there has been a lot of talk and teaching throughout the church about apostles, prophets, and the fivefold ministry of Ephesians chapter 4. It would be easy to just absorb the old teaching about these functions wholesale into simple church, but that would be a huge mistake. The role of apostles and prophets within this movement will probably be as different from what we have known in the past as simple church is from traditional church. In our impatience, we need to be careful that we don't create a new leadership structure that does not reflect God's heart.

The same is true in the area of finances. It would be easy to assume that leaders should receive a salary (and obviously the Scriptures are clear that some should be supported). But in the process, we need to avoid re-creating the clergy/laity divide that has existed for centuries and which is, at heart, a theological as well as a financial issue. In the United Kingdom in the 1970s and 1980s, when thousands of new churches were started across the nation, the local leaders often gave up their secular jobs to be supported by the churches they served. Within a few short years, this led to an elite clergy class of those in full-time ministry. And others, eager to serve the Lord, aspired to the same position. Before long, we were back to a professional clergy.

NEITHER HUMILITY NOR UNITY

Whenever God does something out of the ordinary, humans try to take credit for it. For some time now, we have been praying that God will do something so big in the West that it will be impossible for any one group to claim responsibility. We are watching that happen. What is going on now is on so wide a scale that only God could be responsible, and we need to ask Him to keep us in an attitude of humility, staying low before His cross.

We are also asking Him to keep the church from repeating history. Typically any new move of God is opposed by the move that went before it. We are praying that the legacy churches will joyfully bless and release those who want to get involved in simple churches. And in many situations we are seeing this prayer being answered.

House2House has been very blessed by two megachurches. Leaders of one of them, Northland Church in Orlando, called us to say that they wanted to help the house church movement. We went and spent a day with them, and when they reiterated their desire, we asked them if we could use their video department. They helped us to produce a set of DVDs that has since helped to start churches around the world. The other, Saddleback Church, has used our materials to start house churches within the Hispanic community by translating our *Getting Started Course* into Spanish.

We, in turn, have the responsibility to bless those in the legacy churches we have come from. We should speak well of them and look for ways to cooperatively work together. We are all the body of Christ.

We delude ourselves if we think that simple church is the only thing God is doing across the nation. There are many other wonderful moves of God—examples include prophetic evangelism, the 24-7 prayer movement, the houses of prayer, and the "one new man" Messianic movement. How wonderful it would be if these different strands could braid together to learn from one another.

The longest and most passion-filled prayer of Jesus recorded in the Gospels is His call for unity (John 17). We should be careful not to separate ourselves from our brothers and sisters or think we are somehow better because God is blessing what we are involved in. Many of God's promises are to the church, not to the individual Christian, and the church is all of us, no matter which "family" we belong to. Across the nations, He is clearly blessing and working in every kind of church. We suspect that God is far more concerned with our unity than our correct theology.

PAROCHIALISM

While it is vital that simple churches have an outward focus that reaches out to the people around them, it is also important that they are involved in cross-cultural missions overseas. Opportunities to serve, both long- and short-term, abound. Disciples from simple churches are usually well equipped for missions, and we would do well to encourage them to get involved. Those who travel, especially to Third World countries, will never view life in the same way again. They are often profoundly challenged by the spiritual zeal of those they meet; their hearts are moved with compassion at the poverty and deprivation these brothers and sisters take for granted. When we travel abroad, we frequently take others with us, and we love to watch God change them through the experience.

If we cannot travel ourselves, we can pray. Simple churches could adopt an unreached people group and learn about their way of life and the challenges faced in reaching them. And, of course, we can share some of our material blessings with our brothers and sisters overseas who have so little.

Several years ago there was major flooding in Mozambique. We went out to help with medical relief work, while the networks of simple churches in our city organized a forty-foot container of clothing to be sent out there. The local newspaper did a two-page spread on the medical work, and churches and schools from all over the city took part.

While we were in Mozambique, we camped for a few days in a village square where we ran medical clinics. Every morning, a man dressed in rags raised the Mozambican flag on a flagpole in the middle of the square—a ceremony conducted with great dignity and solemnity. One morning it was raining, and the man was wearing a bright pink woman's raincoat! We knew the people in that community had received a container of clothing!

LEADERS WITHOUT A LIMP

One of the biggest dangers facing this movement is that it will be co-opted by successful leaders. This is not a movement of superstars—their day has passed. It is a movement of ordinary people. It will be tragic if charismatic leaders who have not died to their own ambitions try to take credit for the movement and, in doing so, derail God's work. We need to beware of those with a swollen ego who seek fame, fortune, or control.

God has been preparing leaders for this movement for many years now. You can recognize them because they are broken by years of disappointment and disillusionment; they have experienced tragedies and heartbreaks, financial calamities, and relational disasters. God has been shaping them on His anvil, and they are coming forth as pure gold. These leaders are nobodies, unrecognized by the world and the church. They do not care about their own reputations, only that the glory goes to God. These people are the ones He is choosing to lead this reformation.

A REFORMATION WITHOUT REVIVAL

The changes that are going on through this movement are so fundamental and far reaching that the structure of the church in this country will never be the same again. God is changing the heart of church—transforming her from the inside out—and this change has the potential to be as big as the Reformation. We are not seeking structural change per se. We are looking for Jesus Himself. A new wineskin without new wine is not the answer. If His presence does not permeate what is going on, we have missed the point. The people of God are longing for a fresh experience of Jesus in the midst, and Jesus in the midst *is* church.

Our prayer is that God will deliver the church from these potential challenges so that He can "present her to Himself a glorious church, not having spot or wrinkle or any such thing, but that she should be holy and without blemish" (Ephesians 5:27).

22

NO EMPIRE BUILDING, NO CONTROL, AND NO GLORY

SOME TIME AGO, the Lord gave us a triple slogan that we try to live by: "No empire building, no control, and no glory." None of us is immune to the desire for importance and significance, and it is only by God's grace that any of us can remain humble and unaffected by apparent success.

As this rebirthing of the church continues to unfold, we believe these same three principles should characterize the movement.

NO EMPIRE BUILDING

How easily our focus can switch from building the Kingdom of God to building our own personal kingdoms. As the work of God grows, it is so natural for a person to think he is the indispensable leader and to take the position of CEO—the one who, like King Saul, is head and shoulders above the others. The history of the church is riddled with people like this, who claim ownership of God's work.

Success within simple church movements is not measured by the world's standards. Faithfulness and character are more important in the Kingdom of God. Obedience to the promptings of the Holy Spirit will bring the results we long for. Most of us here in the West do not even count the number of churches that might have started because of our influence. Sometimes people contact us and ask if they can become a House2House church. Our reply to them is that there is nothing to join. We will gladly help them in any way possible, but we are not trying to build a House2House empire.

There will always be people who become well known for their role in God's activities, but we need to pray that these people will be like Jacob and walk with a limp because they know what it is to wrestle with God and to win His favor (Genesis 32). We need to care more about God's Kingdom than our own reputations, dying to ourselves, to our own ambitions and any craving for the limelight. And those who do rise to prominence ought to be ones who are dead to their own desires for power, and who long for God to be glorified above all. Recall Wolfgang Simson's comment about apostolic leadership, "Let them be weeping fathers who seek God—fathers and mothers who long for their sons and daughters to overtake them." Only those with hearts like this can be trusted to lead a movement of God.

NO CONTROL

We all struggle with the temptation to try to control what is going on, often with the very best of intentions. One of the biggest paradigm shifts within the simple church reformation is the understanding that when we are following the Holy Spirit, there is little need for organization and no need for hierarchical control. Ordinary people *can* be entrusted with the affairs of the church, and since Jesus is head of the church, we need to be willing to risk letting the Holy Spirit direct things as He wills. Paul surely faced this many times. Whenever he left a church—sometimes after spending only a few weeks with the people there—he knew he had to trust the ongoing growth of the new believers to the Holy Spirit.

We invited a couple to our home for supper shortly after we met them in one of our meetings. In the middle of the meal, they announced they were starting their own home church the next Sunday. They said a dozen people had already been invited and most had committed to coming.

If they had asked us our opinion first, we might have suggested that they attend our gatherings for a month or two until they had a better understanding of what simple church is about. Perhaps we would have recommended that they go through some kind of training. But since they did not ask us for advice, we blessed them, prayed for them, and offered to help in any way we could. They had about ten not-yet-believers at that first meeting, along with a dozen or so children. A few months later, several were baptized. It is clear that Jesus is building His church. Sometimes it is better when we stay out of the picture!

We so easily could have gotten in the way of what God was

doing by trying to take control. Our motives would have been for quality control. But who is the head of the church? Can we trust Jesus to lead other people without interference from us?

In an article in *Spread the Fire* magazine, John Arnott states, "Seemingly, the Holy Spirit has no problem coordinating hundreds and thousands of different individuals and congregations for His eternal purposes. Things really do work much better when Jesus Himself is the head."[1]

NO GLORY

Isaiah 42:8 (esv) says this: "I am the Lord; that is my name; my glory I give to no other." For humans, the temptation to take just a little bit of the credit is very strong! But it is an incredible privilege to be a part of a move of God, and we need to remember this and stay humble.

When we were still in London, we knew that God was moving powerfully by His Holy Spirit. Thousands of churches were starting in homes all over the country, and many were growing very quickly, even to the point of becoming the largest church in town. Ours was no exception. In just a few years, our attendance had grown considerably, and there was an incredible sense of God's presence every time we met.

One day, Tony overheard two people talking after a meeting. They were commenting about how glad they were to be part of this church rather than another church across town. They talked about how much better our church was, and how much more God was moving within our group than He was in other churches in the area. Tony knew that what they were saying demonstrated a wrong attitude, and yet in his heart he had to admit that he agreed with them. It was just a reflection of the arrogance that had crept into our group. Within a few months, the Lord allowed our church to split right down the middle in a very painful way. As we sought the Lord, trying to figure out why this had happened, we clearly felt that God was dealing with our pride. He could not trust us if we had that kind of attitude. We realized that we dare not risk taking any glory for ourselves or thinking we are better than others.

God can only trust us if we make sure that all the glory goes to Him. He wants simple church to be a grassroots movement of ordinary people, one that does not rely on big names. Like John the Baptist, let's pray that He might increase and we might decrease, and that we go ever lower before the foot of the cross. The only superstar in this movement is the Lord Jesus. We dare not touch His glory. Indeed we desire "no empire building, no control, and no glory"!

23

WHEN SMALL AND BIG WORK TOGETHER

GOD NEVER CEASES to surprise us! A few years ago, within the space of three or four days, we were contacted by three different megachurches interested in either interacting with or learning more about simple/organic churches. God had spoken to Joel Hunter, the senior pastor of Northland: A Church Distributed, in Orlando, telling him clearly that their church was to help partner with others to facilitate the establishment of one million house churches by 2020.[1] The Austin Stone, one of the one hundred fastest-growing churches in the United States, was eager to develop missional communities in Austin, Texas; and the pastor of one of the largest churches in Europe was interested to know more about house churches. Was God up to something?

The ensuing exchange of ideas with these churches cemented a thought that Tony had entertained for several years: What would happen if leaders from both megachurches and microchurches opened a "mega-micro dialogue" and began to brainstorm together? God is obviously blessing both the mega and the micro (and many other legacy churches that don't fall into either category). Is there a way in which we can effectively cooperate with each other?

As leaders from the two different streams came together, it quickly became evident that both groups had much to offer the other, and if we could learn to appreciate the strengths of each, we could partner together for God's Kingdom.

Despite the overall decline of Christianity nationally, simple churches continue to multiply. The number of megachurches and multisite churches is also increasing, and many of the larger churches around the country are showing an interest in the missional principles of simple/organic church. Within denominational circles, many leaders recognize that the demise of an increasing number of legacy churches, exacerbated by the current economic climate, denotes a shift in the church of the future. It's no longer sufficient to do more of the same and do it better. They too are becoming open to experimenting with different models of church.

In 2010, The Austin Stone ran a conference called Verge that attracted people, mainly from legacy and megachurches around the country, to listen to simple/organic church proponents, as well as other speakers with an interest in reaching out via missional communities. The conference sold out in a few weeks, with around two thousand attendees coming to Austin and more than four thousand others participating online.[2] The response was very positive. It seems that many within legacy and megachurches have been waiting and praying for God to do something different. In fact, when recently a Verge Network Web site was launched, featuring talks from the conference, within two weeks the videos were viewed more than 40,000 times![3] In April 2011, Exponential, the largest church-planting conference in the United States, picked up on this momentum.

An increasing number of megachurches are embracing simple church concepts in the form of "missional communities." One missiologist estimates that as many as 60 percent of young Americans will never attend a church service. Legacy churches—even those using a seeker-sensitive approach—are not likely to attract more than 40 percent of those who are open to attending a church service.[4] Missional communities are communities of people on a mission with God, centered on the gospel and reaching out to networks of relationships within a people group or geographical area. The Austin Stone, for example, recognizes that everyone is called by God and can be empowered and sent out into the world—into the coffee shops and neighborhoods, dorms and workplaces—to bear fruit.[5] They ask their people to leave and plant churches. It is not a problem if those who start these missional communities and the people they reach never come to Sunday meetings. They have been released unconditionally to carry out all the functions of church. Perhaps because of this freedom, most of those who have left continue in relationship with the main church, even if they don't attend services.

Northland of Orlando, with their extensive connections, is able to help other legacy churches understand the importance and validity of the microchurch concept. For example, in Central Africa there are 25,000 pastors with no training except for what they receive from megachurches on the prosperity-gospel message. Northland partners with Campus Crusade and its church-led ministries to equip these leaders with house church principles, Bible study programs, and evangelism skills. Already they have trained ninety-six who have started dozens of house churches. They aim to work with two thousand pastors over the next ten years, and as each of those pastors commits to pass on the principles to others, they hope to eventually train at least thirty thousand. The Campus Crusade staff stays connected with these pastors between the semiannual trainings and provides logistical support. House church is the only model that makes financial sense within their context. The megachurch status of Northland gives credibility to the "temple court and house to house" pattern.

When I asked Dr. Dan Lacich, who heads up this work for Northland, what the difference is between a home group of a larger church, or a cell church, and the house churches that are forming, he said, "Each of these simple churches could stand alone as a congregation. They meet weekly in homes for meals, to celebrate communion and to do evangelism, and if feasible, they may be part of a network that has some kind of weekly celebration. The micro needs to be a complete church even if it connects with others for a larger celebration time. If the church is to have greater impact in the world, there may be some things it needs to let go."[6]

Northland has growing numbers of groups that connect with them via the Internet. These groups participate in the service of the main church in their homes, and then following discussion of how to apply the message, serve the community in some way, working with the homeless or doing other kinds of evangelistic activity.

Northland also partners with Global Media Outreach to work in other nations, aiming to eventually work in all twenty of the largest language groups in the world. Individuals from within the church, plus those in churches they partner with from other nations, follow up personally on decisions for Christ made via GMO sites on the Internet. Because most of the new believers are in isolated situations, this involves training them to start simple churches and training them in hospitality and evangelism. The training also connects new believers to resources in their own language and culture.

As megachurches and other denominational churches release their people to start simple churches, the growth of simple/organic churches has the potential to accelerate exponentially. What will it look like if all the churches (mega, denominational, legacy, cell, and simple) partner together to reach their cities and nobody minds who gets the credit?

24

WHERE DO WE GO FROM HERE?

LIFE IS A JOURNEY. The right destination is vital, but life itself is not so much about the destination as the process by which we get there. Simple church is a journey too. We have certainly not arrived—we are merely fellow travelers along with many others on the road. From the very beginning it has been a process of exploring, learning as we go, and doing our best to follow Jesus as He leads us into barely charted territory.

There have been a number of milestones along the highway so far—paradigm shifts in our thinking that have enabled us to change course to follow the spiritual map the Holy Spirit is drawing out of His Word. As we've traveled this path, we've learned several important principles:

- True Christianity is not a weekly event. It's a 24-7, Kingdom lifestyle.
- Jesus is head of His church. He really does speak to His people. We must surrender control of the church to Him.
- Church can be as simple as a group of friends gathering over a meal to share Jesus together.
- We must listen to each other and to the Lord and obey what He says. Both community and mission will result.
- Jesus was not religious.
- Simple is easily reproducible; complex is tough to duplicate.
- Jesus used ordinary, untrained men and women to change the world.
- Leadership is servanthood. We must die to ourselves.
- God's concern is for the harvest. We must ask Him to touch our hearts with the things that are on His heart.
- Jesus said, "Go," and, "As the Father has sent Me, I am sending you."
- The resources are in the harvest.
- It is more effective for the Kingdom to start something in the home of a person of peace with his friends and family than to invite the person of peace to come to your church.
- You can work with a group of not-yet-believers and see them become disciples together—a church!
- Churches are meant to multiply.

For the first time since the beginning of church history, God is changing both the heart and structure of the church on a worldwide scale. Those of us in the West are not the leaders or pioneers in this move of God. That distinction has shifted to those in the Third World, and we would do well to humbly learn from them.

Small is indeed big! Intentionally small churches are here to stay. Enough has gone on beneath the surface and out of sight that they are now unstoppable. They have gone from being dismissed as irrelevant by the church establishment ten or so years ago, to having such an impact on society today that the secular media now take notice of them.[1] There's no going back. The impact they have is out of all proportion to their size. They have the potential to overwhelm everything that is familiar and comfortable. Their influence is already permeating the church establishment to such an extent that denominations and individual churches are taking the principles of simple church seriously. The patterns of outreach Jesus taught His disciples are still relevant today.

Are all simple churches healthy? Will all of them make it? Of course not! But God is taking back His church. He is extending His Kingdom. Intentionally small and simple churches are part of His plan to reach a world that so desperately needs Him.

The King is at work across the nations. There is an explosion of simple churches going on around the world. We have the opportunity of a lifetime to be a part of a move of His Spirit. Imagine coming to the end of our lives only to realize that while God was moving in one direction in our generation, we had chosen a different destination. Intentionally small churches are having a big impact on our world, and the King invites us to join Him in what He is doing.

Appendix

Some Questions and Maybe Some Answers

GOD IS CLEARLY doing something totally new through the simple church movement. Worldwide, small, simple churches are multiplying very quickly. Such a rapidly expanding movement leads to questions, and sometimes there is no definitive scriptural answer. We will give you answers from our own experience and hope that you can learn from our mistakes. In all these situations, you need to follow where the Lord leads you. We tend to think that if the Lord has not spoken clearly through His Word, it is because He wants us to wait in dependency on Him until we hear Him regarding our specific circumstances.

How big should we let our simple church get before we encourage it to multiply?

Most simple church leaders suggest that fifteen to twenty adults is the maximum number for a house church. Although we have had them get to forty or more, a group this large loses the sense of intimacy and makes it nearly impossible for everyone to participate. Again you have to seek the Lord for the answers for your particular situation, but in general, when the numbers get so large that some people stop participating, it is time to multiply.

How do we divide our simple church?

The first church we started grew to more than fifty before we split it down the middle into two groups. For a year after that, people told us that the split felt like a divorce. Because of this, we no longer multiply by dividing a church into two. From the start we encourage anyone who finds a person of peace to seek to start a new church or group within that person's sphere of influence. If, in spite of this, your numbers are reaching a maximum point, rather than include a new family who wants to join in the existing church, try to start a new church around them. Draw on one of the families from the existing church to help. Then it becomes an exciting church plant that the original group takes ownership of and will support. And by doing things this way, you typically have the advantage of moving into a new neighborhood, with a new set of people getting involved.

How do simple churches multiply?

There are four basic ways in which churches can multiply.

1. A community of believers can grow to the point where it has to give birth to a daughter. Here, according to those with experience of rapidly multiplying church plant- ing movements, the shorter the reproduction time (six months is a good length of time), the less likely it is to cause problems for those in the group. An understand- ing of church planting movements will make this a joyful birth rather than a painful divorce.

2. When starting a church in an area or people group where you do not yet know anyone, we recommend using a Luke 10, person of peace, approach. From there, other groups will develop along relational lines.

3. When a new person becomes a believer, start an evangelistic discussion group around that person's circle of family and friends. As more people become disciples, a new church will naturally develop.

4. A group of leaders can be trained to go out and start churches, and then train others to do the same (as in 2 Timothy 2:2). A strategy coordinator with the Southern Baptist church in Cambodia trained six Cambodian leaders over a period of several months. The first year they started six churches. Ten years later, there were over one hundred thousand new believers in the movement that started.[1]

In our experience, it is much more straightforward to start a new work with not-yet-believers. They are overjoyed to find a God who can help them through difficulties and who delights to answer their prayers. Their problems are the problems of life, not issues tied up with their previous church experience. It is easy to go via them to their friends and family.

We often ask the Lord how we can be most strategic within His Kingdom. These days, we find ourselves training others how to make disciples and to start churches more than doing it ourselves. We are learning to multiply ourselves.

Although it is very early yet, the results of a major outreach, such as a citywide crusade, being followed up by simple church methods are extremely encouraging. We've been involved in one situation where the environment is potentially very hostile to the gospel. Yet several major healing and evangelistic meetings have resulted in thousands of new simple churches being formed straight from the harvest. The harvest is not just being conserved but in subsequent months it is multiplying. Other evangelists are now beginning to explore these ideas.

Curtis Sergeant, who spent many years working with house churches in China, describes his strategy for producing multiple generations of churches:

> In church planting it is helpful to keep in mind the training cycle: model, assist, watch, and leave. Generational markers can often serve as a useful guide in knowing when to change roles. That is, the church-planting team model as they plant a church. Then they change roles after the establishment of the church and take an assisting role. They assist the first-generation church in planting a second-generation church. After the second-generation church is planted, they again change roles and begin watching as the second-generation church plants a third-generation church with the assistance of the first-generation church. When this takes place, the church-planting team can transition to start work in a new area, modeling again as they do the work in another first-generation church.[2]

What is a network of churches?

When a group of simple churches relate together, this is usually known as a network. This may happen when a single simple church multiplies out into several churches. It may occur when a traditional church transitions into a number of simple churches. One person or team of people may start several different churches. A group of unrelated churches may find each other and decide to relate together. Often the leaders of the different churches form a leadership team that helps to support and encourage each other and all the churches in the network. This leadership team may include the fivefold ministries of apostles, prophets, evangelists, pastors, and teachers mentioned in Ephesians 4—after all, an individual house church is very unlikely to have this diversity of leadership. The leadership team is not an organizational structure—more a set of friendships. An optimum size for a network is around twelve churches.[3]

As Neil Cole says, we are looking to reproduce disciples, leaders, churches, and movements.[4]

Should all the churches meet together regularly?

When all the churches in a network or group of networks come together for a gathering, this is usually known as a celebration. Church networks differ when it comes to celebrations. Again, it is important to listen to what the Lord is saying for your situation. There are, perhaps, four options:

- Have a regular celebration—many networks do this on a monthly basis.
- Have a celebration only when someone with a message for the whole network of churches is coming into town or if the Lord specifically leads that way.
- Have "mini-celebrations" from time to time where a few simple churches get together in different parts of town.
- Do not have celebrations at all.

Our own experience is worth considering. As our network of simple churches grew, we all met together one Sunday morning a month. We had a worship team, someone would teach, and there was a full program for the kids. But the celebration ran into problems. A number of youth had recently become Christians and we discovered that they did not "do mornings." Additionally, some of the new believers hadn't yet cleaned up their language, and the families who were already Christians, some of whom were also homeschooling their kids, found the four-letter words used in church offensive!

So our leadership team came together to pray about the situation. We decided that the celebrations did not model the values we were trying to portray in simple church, and in addition, the celebrations took a lot of time, energy, and resources. A better pattern might be to bring all the churches together only if there was someone coming to town we wanted everybody to hear.

This had some unforeseen consequences. Many of the long-standing Christian families left. For them, "real church" was the monthly celebration, and they missed all the programs we could offer as a larger group. These families went back to more traditional churches. The people who had become Christians within the simple church context, however, were unfazed. They had wondered why we bothered with celebrations anyway!

What is the relationship between legacy churches and simple churches? Can a legacy church get involved in the simple church movement?

You may be involved in a more traditional church but have gained a vision for starting simple churches with new believers. Can the two be combined?

Alpha groups are a very successful model of evangelism around the world and particularly in the United Kingdom.[5] A group of people, mainly those who are not already involved in church, come together weekly over a ten-week period to share a meal, to listen to some teaching that explains the fundamentals of our faith, and to have a discussion based around questions related to the teaching. At the two weekends away during the course, many of those attending give their lives to Christ and are filled with the Holy Spirit. But problems occur when the course finishes and the leaders try to move people who have become Christians through the small group into traditional churches. The relationships and intimacy developed within this kind of model is the only "church" these new believers know. They frequently cannot cope with a traditional church because they weren't born into it. As a result, many of these new believers never get involved in a legacy church once their Alpha group ends, and the harvest is scattered.[6]

In Luke 5:37-39, Jesus says,

> No one puts new wine into old wineskins; or else the new wine will burst the wineskins and be spilled, and the wineskins will be ruined. But new wine must be put into new wineskins, and both are preserved. And no one, having drunk old wine, immediately desires new; for he says, "The old is better."

New wine needs new wineskins.

If you start new groups, we suggest you don't try to incorporate them into your traditional church. If you are a church leader, view these groups as an outreach of your church. Set them free without conditions, and allow them to grow and multiply without being under your control. You cannot out-give God. If you train and release your people to start these simpler forms of church, God will give back far more than you may lose in terms of manpower or finances. Similarly, if you try to put people who have only known traditional church into house church, many will come back to you saying, "We preferred the old way of doing things."

If you are not in a position of leadership in your church, prayerfully approach the leaders and ask them if they will release you to work in this way as a "local missionary." When ordinary people are released to do the work of the Kingdom, God does the extraordinary!

What is the life cycle of a simple church?

Simple church is like family. Just as children grow up and leave home and get married and have their own families, so it is with house churches, at least in a Western culture. Simple churches are living organisms, passing through various seasons of life. They are born, and they experience growth pains. If they are healthy, they give birth to other churches. Sometimes they get inflicted with a spiritual disease. Eventually they may die, but "unless a grain of wheat falls into the ground and dies, it remains alone; but if it dies, it produces much grain" (John 12:24).

Is this a problem? It is too early in the movement to say. However, death is a natural part of life, and from the death of these churches, new life springs forth. We would rather have a church without the presence of the Holy Spirit be decently buried than maintained on life support indefinitely.

God is clearly doing something, and He is well able to take care of His own reputation.

What problems occur when people transfer from a legacy church?

When people leave a legacy church to start or join a simple church, one of the first things they have to overcome is the feeling of guilt that they are not in church on Sunday morning. This can be surprisingly difficult. However, the joy of being able to sleep in, eat a leisurely breakfast, and enjoy some family time soon replaces the guilt! But even so, many of them may eventually say, "The old wine was better."

Sometimes those coming out of the traditional church have negative feelings and resentments toward the old system. They may have been hurt or disappointed, and for a while, they don't want anything to do with the legacy church. This is a dangerous foundation for beginning a new work of God. Some kind of debriefing process, where one recognizes the value of the past while acknowledging and seeking healing for its shortcomings, may be of help. Once the past is thoroughly dealt with, people can then move on to the new phase that God is leading them into.

Some people refer to the process of leaving as a "detox" time. This may sound somewhat negative to those still involved in a legacy church. However, it is a picture of the issues facing people who have spent their entire life in a more traditional structure. People miss the old. After a while they crave the familiar rituals. There is nothing wrong with this—but it is good to recognize that there may be a cost to leaving the old. It is helpful to have a strong calling from God before embarking on this adventure of simple organic church.

Can a traditional church transition into a network of simple churches?

God is doing all kinds of amazing things with both legacy and simple churches. We are now aware of a number of situations where God has led a legacy church to successfully become a network of house churches. The process has plenty of challenges. Most people who attend a legacy church signed up for a certain form of church, and the changes leave them feeling very insecure. As Jesus said, many people who have tasted the old wine prefer it. There are also questions for the paid staff—how will they be supported if the church transitions? It is best to count the cost before moving ahead (Luke 14:28-32).

In other situations, legacy churches are encouraging their members to start simple churches as a means of outreach. Some denominations, like the Foursquare Church, now have a house church track and see these groups as a viable way of expressing church within their denomination.

God knows your situation! He has a plan that is unique to your circumstances, and He is waiting to reveal His will to you.

For an example of a legacy church that has transformed itself into a network of home churches, go to http://www.apexcommunity.net. For an example of a small church that has transformed itself into a network, go to http://www.bridgepoint.org.

Is it important to have outside input?

Small groups always have a tendency to be somewhat inward looking. Outside input given by visiting ministries such as apostles or prophets provides a healthy balance. In the New Testament it is clear that most new churches were either planted or helped by outside workers who traveled to visit them (Acts 8:14; 11:27). Many of Paul's letters were written to churches in crisis or conflict.

Some members of the body are uniquely gifted to build, nurture, equip, and encourage churches (Ephesians 4:11-16). This can be especially helpful in the event of a problem when someone from the outside may be able to view the situation more objectively.

Training and encouragement are especially important in order for churches to thrive and multiply. We should view those with apostolic or other fivefold gifting and experience as a great resource.

Although churches may develop a strong relationship with certain gifted people, especially if an apostle fathered them, it is also healthy to have a broad spectrum of input from people with differing viewpoints.

Should churches and networks connect together?

In our experience, healthy churches do network together. We also see this in the New Testament where Paul asks the church at Colosse to share his letter to them with the church at Laodicea and vice versa (Colossians 4:16). They were obviously used to cooperating together. The churches did this at a financial level as well (1 Corinthians 16:1-4). This connection can occur at a local, regional, national, or even international level, especially in these days when global communication is so easy. A synergy can be gained from drawing on one another's experiences and strengths.

Social networking sites such as http://www.simplechurch.com are helping on the technical side. They provide a great venue for communication and for forging new relationships.

Is there a leadership structure that connects all these churches?

There is no central organization behind the current movement of organic churches in the West. The individual house churches and networks of churches remain autonomous. But friendships and relationships are deepening across the whole spectrum of the movement with a strong spirit of cooperation between them. We need to pray this unity continues.

There are legitimate concerns, confirmed by recent church history, that most movements of the Holy Spirit eventually coalesce into new denominations. What is to prevent this from happening here? This is a good question, to which there may not be an authoritative answer. But as we look around the world, especially at movements in India and China that are much larger and have a much longer history, we are encouraged that so far, they have been able to keep denominationalism at bay and are still demonstrating an encouraging unity in the Spirit. This is our prayer as these movements continue to develop here in the West.

Does a simple church need a pastor?

The term *pastor* is only used once in the New Testament (Ephesians 4:11). All other uses of *shepherd* (Greek *poimen*) as a noun, apart from the literal ones where sheep are involved, refer to Jesus. (In 1 Peter 5:2, a related word is used when elders are told to feed the flock of God in their care.) The concept of the pastor as we know it in the Western church was unknown in New Testament times.

Simple churches are more like families. Does a family have a leader? Yes—parents are the leaders of families. Simple churches need spiritual fathers and mothers who will lay down their lives for those in their care.

Who "covers" a simple church?

The issue of authority or covering is one that has been used by leaders to gain or retain control over their people. It is not a scriptural concept. In his book *Reimagining Church*, Frank Viola says,

> Take for instance Corinth, the most troubled church mentioned in the New Testament. Throughout the entire Corinthian correspondence, Paul never appeals to the elders. He never chastises them. He never commends obedience to them. In fact, he doesn't even mention them. Instead, Paul appeals to the whole church. He shows that it's the church's responsibility to deal with its own self-inflicted wounds. Paul charges and implores the "brethren" more than thirty times in 1 Corinthians. And he writes as if no officers exist. This is also true for all his other letters to churches in crisis. . . . Notice that Paul's stress is on function, not position. His instruction is placed upon the shoulders of the whole church. The entire book of Corinthians is a plea to the whole assembly to handle its own problems.[7]

The references to human "authority" in the New Testament all refer to city or national governments. There are a couple of references that refer to elders or leaders leading or having authority; Jesus demonstrated how this authority was to function by washing His disciples' feet (John 13:4-17).

What other resources are available?

Many other groups and resources are available to help the movement, including the following:

- House2House Ministries has a Web site (www.house2house.com) with many useful articles and links and also produces resources such as books, DVDs, and conferences.
- http://www.simplechurch.com is a social networking site for those in simple/organic church movements. Many people from around the world are using this site to network with others.
- Church Multiplication Associates runs Greenhouse Trainings—regional conferences to help people start organic churches with an emphasis on working with the lost. (See http://www.cmaresources.org.)
- http://www.LK10.com is a "community of practice" designed to encourage and support church planters.
- http://www.shapevine.com, cofounded by Alan Hirsch, has many useful resources, particularly regarding the transition from attractional to missional church life.
- David Watson's blog, Touchpoint, can be found at http://www.davidwa.org.

Many DVDs are available as well. These include:

- *Tidal Wave*, which describes simple church movements in the West. Available as a DVD or free download at www.house2house.com.
- *When You Come Together* provides very helpful practical insights on simple church gatherings. Available as a DVD or free download at www.house2house.com.
- *UpsideDown Leadership* looks at the whole question of leadership within simple churches. Available as a DVD or free download at www.house2house.com.

We also recommend the following books:

- *An Army of Ordinary People* by Felicity Dale
- *Getting Started* by Felicity Dale
- *Revolution* by George Barna
- *Simply Church* by Tony and Felicity Dale
- *Church 3.0* by Neil Cole
- *Organic Church* by Neil Cole
- *Organic Leadership* by Neil Cole
- *Search and Rescue* by Neil Cole
- *Housechurch 101* by Wolfgang Simson
- *Nexus* by Rad Zdero
- *The Global House Church Movement* by Rad Zdero
- *The Church Comes Home* by Rob and Julia Banks
- *Church Planting Movements* by David Garrison
- *Pagan Christianity?* by Frank Viola and George Barna
- *Reimagining Church* by Frank Viola
- *Jesus Has Left the Building* by Paul Vieira

- *MegaShift* by James Rutz
- *The Shaping of Things to Come* by Michael Frost and Alan Hirsch

Acknowledgments

OVER THE YEARS we have had the privilege of sharing in the lives of others who have far more extensive experience than we do with the issues covered in this book. We have spent hours discussing the different ways God is working. We have spoken on regular, extended conference calls; we have lingered over meal tables together; and we have spent days listening to God together. These "iron sharpening iron" times have helped to shape our thinking.

We value and appreciate the wisdom of people like Victor and Bindu Choudhrie, Neil Cole, Curtis Sergeant, Wolfgang Simson, Mike Steele, and John White.

Other friends have also blazed a trail that we have been privileged to walk along: Robert Fitts, Alan Hirsch, Jim Rutz, Frank Viola.

Finally, our thanks go out to all those who were willing to share their stories from the trenches in the pages of this book.

Notes

INTRODUCTION

1. As far as we can determine, this story originated with Curtis Sergeant, who has extensive personal experience of rapidly growing church planting movements throughout the world. It was popularized by Wolfgang Simson, a church growth specialist and researcher from Germany.

CHAPTER 1

1. Frank Viola, *From Eternity to Here* (Colorado Springs: David C. Cook, 2009), 230–231.
2. This was a nationwide telephone survey conducted during December 2007 among a random sample of 1,005 adults living within the forty-eight continental states.

CHAPTER 2

1. The Karis Group is based in Austin, TX, and focuses on helping those who are uninsured or underinsured deal with their medical bills when the bills exceed the resources or benefits that they have available. For more information see the company Web site, www.thekarisgroup.com.
2. This quote has been attributed to C. Peter Wagner.
3. Examples include *Leaves of Healing* in the healing movement of the late nineteenth century, *Fullness* and *Restoration* magazines in the British house church movement, and *New Wine* in the charismatic movement here in the United States.

CHAPTER 3

1. Historical information for this chapter comes from The Friends of William Tyndale, "The Amazing Story behind the Making of the English Bible," http://www.williamtyndale.com; Wikipedia, s.v. "William Tyndale," http://en.wikipedia.org/wiki/William_Tyndale.

2. J. H. Merle d'Aubigne, *History of the Reformation in Europe in the Time of Calvin*, vol. 5, *England, Geneva, Ferrara* (New York: Robert Carter & Brothers, 1880), 228–229.

3. Clay Shirky, *Here Comes Everybody: The Power of Organizing without Organizations* (New York: The Penguin Press, 2008), 67–68.

4. A great social networking site for simple church can be found at http://www.simplechurch.com.

5. See *Tidal Wave*, a DVD available for purchase at http://www.house2house.com.

CHAPTER 4

1. For an interesting treatise on this subject see *The Pilgrim Church* by E. H. Broadbent (Port Colborne, ON: Gospel Folio Press, 2002).

2. Curtis Sergeant, who has extensive church planting experience in China, says this about the house church movement in that country: "Mr. Ye Xiaowen, the director of China's State Administration of Religious Affairs (the highest Communist Party official in charge of all religious affairs), in two meetings at Beijing University and in the China Academy of Social Sciences, claimed the number of Christians in China, including both the underground and the government-sanctioned churches, both Catholic and Protestant, has reached 130 million members. A lot of people now cite those figures. There is a reasonable chance that there is some overlap among those groups. I personally use a number of 100 million, seeking to compensate for some of the overlap and to take out a percentage of the Catholics, some of which may not be born again." From an e-mail message to Felicity Dale, July 22, 2008.

3. Wolfgang Simson, ed., "The World's Largest Churches," DAWN Fridayfax 2004 #36, Jesus Fellowship Church, http://www.jesus.org.uk/dawn/2004/dawn36.html.

4. David Haldane, "Seeking the Living Word—In Their Living Rooms—It's How the Church Began, Say Small Christian Groups That Forgo Clergy and Ritual," *Los Angeles Times*, July 23, 2007; Rita Healy, "Why Home Churches Are Filling Up," *Time*, February 27, 2006, http://www.time.com/time/magazine/article/0,9171,1167737,00.html.

5. This data is from surveys conducted in early 2008 among a national random sample of 2,009 adults living in the forty-eight continental states. To gauge

house church attendance, the following question was used in the Barna Group survey: "Some people are part of a group of believers that meets regularly in a home or place other than a church building. These groups are not part of a typical church; they meet independently, are self-governed, and consider themselves to be a complete church on their own. Do you participate in such a group, sometimes known as a house church or simple church, that is not part of a local, congregational type of church? (If yes, ask:) How often do you, personally, attend the meetings of that group? At least once a week, 2 or 3 times a month, once a month, or less than once a month?"

6. The Barna Group conducted this survey by telephone in November 2007 among a nationwide random sample of 615 head ministers or senior pastors of Protestant churches in the forty-eight continental states.

7. Steve Sells, "Diagnostics," Transformational Ministries, http://www.transformationalministries.net/diagnostics.html.

8. John Dart, "Stressed Out: Why Pastors Leave," *Christian Century*, November 29, 2003, http://www.pulpitandpew.duke.edu/Stressed.htm.

9. See John Eldredge's books *Wild at Heart* (Nashville: Thomas Nelson, 2001) and *Waking the Dead* (Nashville: Thomas Nelson, 2003).

10. Alan Jaimieson, "Ten Myths about Church Leavers," *Reality*, http://www.reality.org.nz/articles/32/32-jamieson.html.

11. Reggie McNeal, *The Present Future* (San Francisco: Jossey-Bass, 2003), 4.

12. See http://www.house2house.com.

13. See *An Army of Ordinary People* by Felicity Dale for stories of this phenomenon.

CHAPTER 5

1. Michael Frost and Alan Hirsch, *The Shaping of Things to Come* (Peabody, MA: Henrickson Publishers, 2003); Pete Ward, *Liquid Church* (Peabody, MA: Hendrickson Publishers, 2002).

2. Alan Hirsch, *The Forgotten Ways* (Grand Rapids, MI: Brazos Press, 2006), 36–37.

3. Ward, *Liquid Church*.

CHAPTER 6

1. Bethel Church in Redding, California, would be an example of this. Bill Johnson, the senior pastor, has written several books that document some of these miracles.

2. The International House of Prayer in Kansas City uses music integrated into prayer in continuous worship, intercession, and warfare—commonly known as "Harp and Bowl."

3. See http://www.24-7prayer.com.

4. Well-known British leader Gerald Coates wrote a book entitled *Non-Religious Christianity* (Shippensburg, PA: Destiny Image Publishers, 1998) that expands on these principles.

CHAPTER 7

1. An excellent resource for understanding more fully how to "hear God's voice" are the writings of Mark Virkler as well as John Eldredge's book *Walking with God*.
2. For a discussion on the baptism in the Holy Spirit we suggest that you see http://en.wikipedia.org/wiki/Baptism_with_the_Holy_Spirit.
3. John White, e-mail message to Felicity Dale, July 30, 2008.

CHAPTER 8

1. Full Gospel Central Church was started in 1958 by Dr. David (Paul) Yonggi Cho and his mother-in-law, Choi Ja-shil.
2. According to the World Values Surveys, between 1982 and 2001 the number of Christians in South Korea increased from 23.5 percent of the population to 39.3 percent. "Religious Demographic Profile: South Korea," The Pew Forum on Religion and Public Life, http://pewforum.org/world-affairs/countries/?CountryID=194.
3. "Breakfast with David Yonggi Cho and Rick Warren," Pastors.com, 2001, http://legacy.pastors.com/rwmt/article.asp?ArtID=578.
4. Denny Kenaston, "The Radical Chinese House Churches," *The Heartbeat of the Remnant*, January/February 2003; Kenaston, "The Radical Chinese House Churches, Part 2," *Remnant*, March/April 2003, http://www.charityministries.org/theremnant/theremnant-textonly.a5w.
5. David Watson, "Church Planting Essentials—Prayer," Touch Point: David Watson's Blog, December 27, 2007, http://www.davidwa.org/node/27.

CHAPTER 9

1. Wolfgang Simson, *Houses that Change the World*, (Emmelsbüll, Germany: C & P Publishing, 1999), 80–89.
2. Jared Looney, post on LK10.com, http://lk10.com/component/option,com_fireboard/ltemid,31/func,view/catid,20/id746/.

CHAPTER 10

1. See the DVD *When You Come Together*, available for purchase at www.house2house.com.
2. Frank Viola, *Gathering in Homes* (Gainesville: Present Testimony Ministry, 2006), 29–31.

3. Academic Skills Center, "Active Study," Dartmouth College, http://www.dartmouth.edu/~acskills/docs/study_actively.doc.
4. David Watson, CPM Awareness videos, http://feeds2.feedburner.com/cpmtr.

CHAPTER 12

1. David B. Barrett, Todd M. Johnson, Christopher Guidry, and Peter Crossing, *World Christian Trends, AD 30 to AD 2200*, (Pasadena, CA: William Carey Library, 2001), 520–29.
2. Neil is founder of Church Multiplications Associates, which trains people in discipling and leadership through Greenhouse Trainings. He has written several great books including *Organic Church* (San Francisco: Jossey-Bass, 2005), *Search and Rescue* (Grand Rapids: Baker Books, 2008), and *Organic Leadership* (Grand Rapids: Baker Books, 2009).
3. George Patterson, "Basic Commands of Christ," Mentor and Multiply, http://www.mentorandmultiply.com.

CHAPTER 13

1. Jared Looney, post on LK10.com, http://lk10.com/component/option,com_fireboard/Itemid,31/func,view/catid,20/id746/.
2. This definition is found in the DVD *Like a Mighty Wave*, produced by the International Mission Board of the Southern Baptist Convention.
3. For a fuller discussion on this, see David Garrison's excellent book *Church Planting Movements* (Midlothian, VA: WIGTake Resources, 2004).
4. A good example of this is the work being done by Neil Cole and Church Multiplication Associates.
5. For more on this, see David Garrison's *Church Planting Movements*.
6. John White is involved in a Web site at http://www.LK10.com that provides a "community of practice" for church planters. The 10:2b virus is an integral part of what they do.

CHAPTER 15

1. David Garrison, *Church Planting Movements* (Midlothian VA: WIGTake Resources, 2004), 286–291.

CHAPTER 16

1. The Barna Group conducted a study on people's perceptions and pursuit of holiness in January 2006 by interviewing 1,003 randomly selected adults in the forty-eight continental states. The survey did show that born-again Christians were more likely than other adults to believe that God expects them to become holy, but only a minority (46 percent) of them held that view.

2. This is based on a nationwide survey of 1,006 adults randomly sampled and interviewed in January 2008.

3. Curtis Sergeant, "Insights from a CPM Practitioner," SAM Region Resource Site, http://www.wsaresourcesite.org/Files/CPMs/CLS-CPM%20mss.doc.

4. Neil Cole, *Cultivating a Life for God* (Carol Stream, IL: ChurchSmart Resources, 1999).

5. Kent Smith, "The Dawn Texas Project: A Harvest Force Report," (private research project, 2003–2004).

CHAPTER 17

1. For more on this aspect of leadership, read Neil Cole's excellent book *Organic Leadership* (Grand Rapids: Baker Books, 2009).

2. From a talk given by Wolfgang Simson at our home in 2001.

3. There are two verses that address this subject. Acts 14:23 (NLT) describes how Paul and Barnabas returned to the churches they had started and appointed elders "turn[ing] the elders over to the care of the Lord, in whom they had put their trust." However, in Titus 1:5, Titus is instructed to appoint elders in every city.

4. Ephesians 2:20, NLT. It is beyond the scope of this book to explore the role of apostles and prophets, elders and deacons, in any depth.

CHAPTER 18

1. According to Curtiss Paul DeYoung, Professor of Reconciliation Studies at Bethel University and coauthor of *United by Faith* (New York: Oxford University Press), only about 5 percent of the nation's churches are racially integrated. He defines racially integrated as having at least 20 percent of the membership belonging to a racial group other than the predominant one within that church.

2. This is based on interviews conducted by The Barna Group with 2,009 adults randomly sampled from across the nation. In total, about 5 percent of adults attended a simple church gathering at least once during a typical month during the first half of 2008. Whereas just under 9 percent of black adults had done so, 6 percent of Hispanic adults and 4 percent of white adults participated in simple church activities. Projected nationally, an estimated 11 million adults had a house church experience in the first half of 2008.

3. These figures are drawn from PastorPoll™, a national tracking study conducted by The Barna Group among the senior pastors of Protestant churches. This average comes from three waves of the tracking study conducted in November 2007, December 2007, and August 2008, among a random sample of 1,833 senior pastors.

4. Angus Kinnear, *Against the Tide: The Story of Watchman Nee* (Eastbourne, Sussex, UK: Victory Press, 1973), 172.

5. I (Felicity) would like to add a couple of caveats. First, Tony was always very supportive and encouraged me to do anything I sensed the Lord laying on my heart. It was the system that was oppressive to women. Incidentally that group of churches in the United Kingdom has totally changed and now spearheads a move toward equality for women within the church. Secondly, not all women have the same passions and desires that I do, and that is fine. And please do not think I am blaming the men for this. They were seeking to obey the Scriptures too.

6. Some people say that Junia was actually "Junias" (a man's name). According to British theologian Martin Scott, Junia was a very common woman's name. According to P. Lampe, there are over 250 contemporary references to Junia and not one single one to Junias. James D. G. Dunn, *Word Biblical Commentary*, vol. 38b, *Romans 9–16*, (Nashville: Thomas Nelson, 1988), 894.

7. Iris Ministries homepage; Administration, Iris Ministries, Inc., http://www.irismin.com/.

8. This saying was first used by A. W. Tozer in his book of essays entitled *That Incredible Christian*.

CHAPTER 19

1. Todd Johnson, "World Christian Trends 2005," LausanneWorldPulse.com, November 2005, http://www.lausanneworldpulse.com/trendsandstatistics/11-2005.

2. Wolfgang Simson, "Organic Church Finances" (lecture, Organic Church Movements Conference, Long Beach, CA, February 8–10, 2008).

3. John W. Kennedy, "The Debt Slayers," *Christianity Today*, May 1, 2006, http://www.christianitytoday.com/ct/2006/may/23.40.html.

4. John Wesley, "The Use of Money," Thomas Jackson, ed., Global Ministries: The United Methodist Church, http://new.gbgm-umc.org/umhistory/wesley/sermons/50/.

5. Sondra Higgins Matthaei, "Rethinking Faith Formation," *Religious Education*, Winter 2004, http://findarticles.com/p/articles/mi_qa3783/is_200401/ai_n9358422/pg_9.

6. See http://www.crown.org.

7. See http://www.conceptsinstewardship.org.

8. See http://www.daveramsey.com/fpu/home.

9. Bill Hoffman, "Can It Be That Simple?" House2House.com, January 28, 2009, http://www.story.house2house.com/can-it-be-that-simple/.

CHAPTER 20

1. This concept comes from a book entitled *The Tipping Point: How Little Things Can Make a Big Difference* by Malcolm Gladwell (New York: Back Bay Books, 2000).
2. The Web site http://www.LK10.com is a community of people designed to coach one another.
3. From a talk given by Wolfgang Simson.
4. The heading for this section, a play on the title of the movie *Honey, I Shrunk the Kids*, was coined by our friend John White of www.LK10.com.
5. Neil Cole, *Organic Church* (San Francisco: Jossey-Bass, 2005), 115–116.
6. Aaron Snow, "Extreme Make-over," House2House.com, January 28, 2009, http://www.story.house2house.com/extreme-make-over/.

CHAPTER 21

1. The books *When Heaven Invades Earth: A Practical Guide to a Life of Miracles* and *The Supernatural Power of a Transformed Mind: Access to a Life of Miracles* (Shippensburg, PA: Destiny Image Publishers, 2005) by Bill Johnson of Bethel Church in Redding, California, express the concept well.

CHAPTER 22

1. John Arnott, "Let's Get Back to Supernatural Church!" *Spread the Fire*, no. 5, 2004, http://www.tacf.org/Portals/0/stf%2010-5.pdf.

CHAPTER 23

1. This is captured in an article in *Charisma* magazine that describes Northland's role; http://www.northlandchurch.net/blogs/the_church_dropout.
2. The information on Verge and The Austin Stone comes from a telephone conversation with our friend Michael "Stew" Stewart, pastor of missional community at The Austin Stone and founder/director of the Verge Network and Conference.
3. http://www.vergenetwork.org
4. These ideas come from Alan Hirsch, a South Africa–born missiologist who lived most of his life in Australia and who has a profound influence on many of these churches, encouraging them to become more missional. The term *missional* means that people from the church go out into their communities with the Good News of Jesus, as compared to attractional churches (like those with a seeker-sensitive emphasis), which invite people to come to church.
5. http://www.austinstone.org/what/missional_communities
6. From a conversation with Dr. Dan Lacich, pastor of distributed sites at Northland: A Church Distributed, in Orlando, Florida.

CHAPTER 24

1. "House of Worship: More Americans Attend Home Services," http://www
.msnbc.msn.com/id/3032619/ns/nightly_news/#39787679; "Growing
Movement of Christians Skip the Sermon, Worship in Small Groups at
Home," http://www.foxnews.com/us/2010/07/21/
growing-movement-christians-skip-sermon-worship-small-groups-home.

APPENDIX

1. From the DVD *Like a Mighty Wave*, produced by the International Mission
Board of the Southern Baptist Convention.
2. Curtis Sergeant, "Insights from a CPM Practitioner," South America Region
Resource Site, http://www.wsaresourcesite.org/Topics/cpm.htm.
3. From a personal conversation with Curtis Sergeant, who has extensive
experience with church planting movements.
4. "Welcome to Church Multiplication Associates," CMAResources.org, http://
www.cmaresources.org.
5. An estimated eleven million have attended an Alpha course worldwide.
"Welcome," AlphaUSA, http://www.alphausa.org/Groups/1000016933/
What_is_Alpha.aspx.
6. In the United Kingdom, where Alpha was started, research shows that if
traditional churches run Alpha over a number of years, they may not decline
as rapidly as churches that do not run Alpha, and may even start to grow
from Alpha. Mike Booker and Mark Ireland, *Evangelism—Which Way Now?*
(London: Church House Publishing, 2007), 14–16.
7. Frank Viola, *Reimagining Church* (Colorado Springs: David C. Cook,
2008), 183.

Tony *&* Felicity Dale

Tony and Felicity Dale would love to keep in touch with you and let you know about other resources that they have produced. These resources include a regular e-letter that goes out to people around the world, as well as DVDs that help to explain more fully what simple church movements look like in practice.

For more information, please visit
www.tonyandfelicitydale.com.

CP0322

an **army** of
ORDINARY
PEOPLE

stories of real-life men and women
SIMPLY BEING THE CHURCH

FELICITY DALE

foreword by GEORGE BARNA

978-1-4143-2279-7

In *An Army of Ordinary People,* renowned church planter Felicity Dale shares stories of how God has always used—and is still using—ordinary believers to carry out his work in simple ways throughout the world. Some of these stories are dramatic—people being led to the Lord by the friends who counseled them through drug addictions and criminal pasts. Some are everyday—a dad spending his Sunday teaching Bible lessons to his kids or a couple inviting their neighbors over for dinner and a spiritual discussion. But in each story, there is a lightbulb moment, when someone just like you thinks, *I can do that!* And as a result, the gospel is spreading . . . and lives are being changed.

Barna Books encourage and resource committed believers seeking lives of vibrant faith—and call the church to a new understanding of what it means to be the Church.

For more information, visit www.tyndale.com/barnabooks.

BARNA

CP0309